W9-BZU-857

7
7/22
SS

TIMELESS

SUPER

achievers

TIMELESS

SUPER

achievers

TESTED
STRATEGIES FOR
SUCCESS FROM
SELLING POWER
MAGAZINE

Timeless Superachievers

Copyright © 1998 by Gerhard Gschwandtner

All rights reserved. Printed in the U.S.A.

No part of this book may be reproduced or copied in any form without

written permission from the publisher.

Timeless Superachievers is published in the United States by

Personal Selling Power Inc., P.O. Box 5467, Fredericksburg, VA 22403

Phone 540/752-7000

www.sellingpower.com

Book and jacket designed by Jen Linch

Library of Congress Catalog Card # 98-067886

ISBN# 0-939613-15-8

ACKNOWLEDGMENTS

The publisher wishes to thank the many professionals who contributed their time and efforts to make this book a useful and valuable tool. These include, first, the superachievers whose lives and work lessons are included here. Next, the writers, editors and designers who brought those lessons to the printed page. Laurie Ross who proofread the pages, Jen Linch whose patient, creative spirit gave form to the book, Tarver Harris for extra production work, Dana Ray who located, wrote and created many extra pieces to enhance the experience of reading for the user, Jeff Macharyas who kept the process on schedule and Terry Frimmet who added final copy to help move the book off the shelves and into people's hands and hearts.

HOW TO USE THIS BOOK

In 1990* *Selling Power* magazine published ground-breaking research on the traits and habits of superachievers. The study, conducted by *Selling Power* and Dr. Seymour Epstein of The University of Massachusetts at Amherst, clearly defined what superachievers do on a daily basis to outperform average achievers. In this book, you can read about how such superachievers plan, work, think and grow in their professional lives. While you read the book, you can make notes, examine your own achievement patterns and begin to model your professional growth on patterns that have proven effective for these outstanding men and women. Yes, they all started with talent. But many seemed only average when they began their careers. Over time, they proved that hard work, discipline, attitude, motivation and a determination to try new ways of thinking to overcome problems can actually make a substantial difference in outcomes. We hope this book will help readers grow beyond self-imposed limits and reach new heights of accomplishment in their professional lives.

* *The articles in this book were originally published in* Selling Power *magazine between 1986 and 1996.*

table of contents

NEARLY HALF A CENTURY AFTER HIS DEATH,

DALE CARNEGIE'S TIMELESS TEACHINGS CAN STILL

HELP YOU WIN SALES AND INFLUENCE BUYERS.

Dale Carnegie

The Brooklyn businessman, newly enrolled in a Dale Carnegie course, approached the podium to deliver his maiden speech. To this day, people recall how his hands trembled and his face twitched. Reaching the lectern, the Brooklyner turned to face his listeners. He felt like a man under a 1,000-watt bulb. He unhinged his jaw, but nothing came out. He fainted and crumpled to the floor. In an instant, Dale Carnegie leapt to the platform and swept his hand toward the prostrate body.

"One month from today, this man will make a speech from this platform!" he thundered.

Sure enough, one month later the famous Brooklyn fainter made that speech.

Dale Carnegie – who was this man who inspired hundreds of thousands, and whose message has blossomed and spread in the 30 years since his death in 1955 to help mold millions of men and women including now-legendary figures like Lee Iacocca, Zig Ziglar and Ed Foreman?

> ## fascinating fact
>
> *Initially, the YMCA refused to pay Dale Carnegie even five dollars a night salary.*

Like all those who earn "bigger than life" status, Carnegie was many people in one: salesman, brilliant intellect, grassroots philosopher, renowned speaker and innovator, and author of the worldwide bestseller *How to Win Friends and Influence People*. A diligent scholar familiar with Shakespeare, Socrates and Plato. A pragmatist who applied learning to advance his teachings. Friend of presidents, explorers, film stars, writers and the common man. Equally comfortable in the company of business leaders or heads of state.

More than anything else, Carnegie was a man who believed – and proved

9

countless times over – that the art of communication, learned through the mastery of public speaking and the study of human nature, is the key to prosperity and happiness.

THE MAN

J. Oliver Crom, who met Carnegie in 1952 and is now president of Dale Carnegie & Associates Inc. in New York, remembers him as a person with innumerable interests, a deep love of life and a wonderful sense of humor.

"He loved to work in the yard. He was a gardener and loved roses. He was a fantastic photographer and he loved the theater. He loved museums. He loved everything in life – fishing and hunting and climbing mountains," says Crom.

fascinating fact

For a while, Carnegie lived in a roach-infested furnished room on West 56th Street in New York City.

"He asked questions and listened." In other words, Carnegie practiced what he preached in his famous book and lectures; he showed appreciation for people, made them feel important and respected the views of others.

Crom has a favorite story that illustrates this quality of Carnegie's:

"He was at a very fancy affair, and was seated next to a scientific person. Mr. Carnegie knew nothing about this particular science, but throughout the dinner he asked the scientist questions that encouraged him to talk about what he was involved in. At the end of the dinner, the scientist went up to the host and told him that Mr. Carnegie was a most fascinating conversationalist – and all that he'd done was ask questions and listen!"

The idea of showing appreciation for others through intent listening was first outlined in Carnegie's lecture (and later book) *How to Win Friends and Influence People*. The book, which has since been printed in nearly 40 languages, made Carnegie an "overnight" success. Of course, like most "overnight" successes, Carnegie's triumph took many years to achieve – 24, in fact. During that time, Carnegie developed the ideas that would later form the hub of his teachings. Through an incredible variety of jobs, experiences and travels, he molded himself into the man who would one day have the ears of millions.

THE MYTH

Like Abe Lincoln, whom he admired (and later wrote a book about), Carnegie had a background from which myths are made – both came from humble origins. Born in 1888, son of an unsuccessful Missouri hog farmer, young Dale rode to school on horseback wearing a pair of pants that pinched and a coat that swallowed him. But even as a youth, he shot off sparks illuminating the brilliant career that lay ahead. In college he so excelled at debating that he was given the job of coaching other members of the debate team.

Beginning in 1908, Carnegie took jobs selling everything from bacon to courses in engineering. He gave up selling temporarily to tour the country as an actor and stage manager. Disappointed with his income, Carnegie augmented his earnings by selling neckties, then chucked both to sell Packard automobiles, a product he amiably admitted he "knew nothing about."

Carnegie's turnaround year was 1912. It was then that he hit on the idea of teaching a course on public speaking at New York City's YMCA. The course was a smash hit, as were the inspirational articles he began to publish. By 1916, he was earning $400 per week, big money for those days, and could call on the likes of Franklin D. Roosevelt, then Navy Secretary, to headline a speaking engagement.

Already, Carnegie was beginning to understand why audiences were drawn to him. "Those adults didn't come to my classes because they wanted college credit or social prestige," Carnegie later recalled. "They wanted to solve their problems. They wanted to be able to stand up on their feet and say a few words at a business meeting without fainting from fright."

At the same time, Carnegie discovered the technique for getting people to overcome their fear of public speaking. He simply asked them to talk about themselves. "Without knowing what I was doing, I stumbled on the best method of conquering fear," he said.

World War I sidetracked him with a brief Army stint. Afterward, he was off on yet another venture, traveling the globe as Lowell Thomas' business manager. Passing his 30th year, he left Thomas and set out to become a literary legend. However, his novel *Blizzard* was received frostily by publishers.

Like many superachievers, Dale Carnegie was a man leaping from success to success, over the occasional sinkhole of disappointment. He seemed obsessed

Dale Carnegie On Self-Consciousness There is only one person who can cure someone of self-consciousness and that is himself. I know of no other handicap the cure for which can be written in so few words — "Forget yourself." When you are feeling shy, timid, self-conscious, put your mind on something else immediately. If you are speaking, forget everything but the subject. Never mind what others are thinking of you or your delivery; just forget yourself and go ahead.

On Pep Talks Is giving yourself a pep talk every day silly, superficial, childish? No. On the contrary, it is the very essence of sound psychology. "Our life is what our thoughts make it." Those words are just as true today as they were 18 centuries ago when Marcus Aurelius first wrote them in his book of Meditations.

achievement
LESSONS

On Opening Minds Remember that the man you are talking to is a hundred times more interested in himself and his wants and his problems than he is in you and your problems. His toothache means more to him than a famine in China that kills a million people. A boil on his neck interests him more than 40 earthquakes in Africa. Think of that the next time you start a conversation.

On Enthusiasm How can you make yourself become enthusiastic? By telling yourself what you like about what you are doing and passing on quickly from the part you don't like to the part you do like. Then act enthusiastic; tell someone about it; let them know why it interests you.

On Acting If you act "as if" you are interested in your job, that bit of acting will tend to make your interest real. It will also tend to decrease your fatigue, your tensions and your worries.

On Perspective About 90 percent of the things in our lives are right and about 10 percent are wrong. If we want to be happy, all we have to do is concentrate on the 90 percent that are right and ignore the 10 percent that are wrong. If we want to be worried and bitter and have stomach ulcers, all we have to do is to concentrate on the 10 percent that are wrong and ignore the 90 percent that are glorious.

On Enemies When we hate our enemies, we are giving them power over us; power over our sleep, our appetites, our blood pressure, our health and our happiness. Our enemies would dance with joy if only they knew how they were worrying us, lacerating us and getting even with us! Our hate is not hurting them at all, but our hate is turning our own days and nights into a hellish turmoil.

On Selling Ideas Don't you have much more faith in ideas that you discover for yourself than in ideas that are handed to you on a silver platter? If so, isn't it bad judgment to try to ram your opinions down the throats of other people? Wouldn't it be wiser to make suggestions — and let the other man think out the conclusion for himself?

On Worry If you have a worry problem, do these three things:
1. Ask yourself, "What is the worst that can possibly happen?"
2. Prepare to accept it if you have to.
3. Then calmly proceed to improve on the worst.

On Making Friends If you want to win friends, make it a point to remember them. If you remember my name, you pay me a subtle compliment; you indicate that I have made an impression on you. Remember my name and you add to my feeling of importance.

with launching boldly into new ventures, totally undaunted by the prospect of failure, as if for no other reason than to enrich his life with novel experiences. One might surmise that Carnegie sensed the coming calling of his destiny, and that he considered all challenges simply as prerequisite courses.

The stories from this era testify to his exuberant attitude in dealing with roadblocks. There was the time, for instance, that he climbed a telephone pole to sell an engineering course to a lineman. Later selling pork for Armour, Carnegie confronted a merchant who couldn't pay his bill. They struck a bargain. Carnegie took a stack of shoes off the counter, walked down the street to the railway station and sold them to the gandy dancers. The receipts were forwarded to Armour that afternoon.

Each experience – as a salesman, actor, business manager, author – contributed to the man who blossomed during the 1920s.

THE MESSAGE

In 1922 he again began to teach, patiently building up his classes in New York. Not discouraged by the failure of his novel, Carnegie resumed writing, turning out innumerable articles and publishing his first successful book, *Lincoln the Unknown*. Soon he was broadcasting his own radio program to millions of listeners.

After several years of teaching, and the 1926 publication of a four-volume work on oratory, Carnegie condensed what he'd learned about his students. It dawned on him that the goal of communication since the eras of Pericles and Cicero had been to influence others. And the most effective communicators had always been those who were not merely good orators, but who also understood human nature.

For Carnegie, it was a revelation. The years of experience crystallized into the seed of what was to become the famous Dale Carnegie Course.

Setting out to learn all he could about the art of human relations, Carnegie was amazed to discover that there wasn't a single modern book on the subject. Ever the man to take the initiative, he hired a researcher who spent eight hours a day for 18 solid months plowing through countless thousands of magazine articles – reading everything that had the remotest bearing on the subject of how to win friends and influence people.

Drawing on this raw material and his own rich experience, Carnegie wrote a brief talk, which later evolved into a full-blown lecture entitled "How to Win Friends and Influence People." A Simon & Schuster editor who happened to take the course liked Carnegie's ideas so much he offered him a book contract. The year was 1936, smack in the middle of the Great Depression. Lines of people jamming bookstores for Carnegie's masterpiece may have at times surpassed those at soup kitchens. A half-million copies sold in the first year.

What made the book such a sensation? Carnegie employed a sure-fire formula: Tell the people something that is practical, personal and optimistic. Keep it simple, and make the goals accessible by using real life stories as proof that the teachings work. It was a winning formula and it worked.

Carnegie taught one fundamental lesson: how to deal successfully with others. He trumpeted the principles of how to be a good salesman of products, services and ideas.

He made his points unforgettable by telling a story and summing it up with a moral. Whether he was quoting Shakespeare or spinning a yarn about a salesman, he employed simple language to reinforce universal principles.

This was his genius – drawing attention to the overlooked nugget of truth. What could be more commonplace than his advice, "Don't criticize, condemn or complain," or "Become genuinely interested in other people"? Where Carnegie was profound, it was in his ability to convince people that these gems of wisdom were too often taken for granted.

TIME-TESTED PRINCIPLES

Because Carnegie was a man of action, it's little wonder that his books are "action books" and his lectures "calls to action." *How to Win Friends and Influence People* proceeds from anecdote to anecdote. In case you missed it, Carnegie offers a one-sentence synopsis at the end of each chapter that tells you what to do.

"If you want to persuade someone to your point of view, make him feel like somebody," said Carnegie. Put yourself in his shoes. Don't talk – listen to his problems and concerns. Show that you are genuinely interested. Don't argue – respect the opinions of others. Lavish praise for the merest achievement or improvement. Make people happy about helping you. In other words, use the personal touch – that's the way to sell yourself.

Carnegie taught that anyone could learn and follow these ideas, and went further to say that all successful people do exactly that. In fact, knowledge of human nature is always more important than mere professional or technical skill. The man who masters this wisdom becomes the trusted steward of power.

Carnegie's principal hero in this regard was Charles Schwab, the man chosen by industrialist Andrew Carnegie to run U.S. Steel. Acknowledged as the first executive to earn a million dollars a year, Schwab frequently admitted that there were many men better versed in the steel business. But he gave ground to no one in the field of human relations, where he was an undisputed master.

In his teachings, Dale Carnegie often used a favorite quote of Schwab's: "I consider my ability to arouse enthusiasm among my people the greatest asset I possess, and the way to develop the best that is in a person is by appreciation and encouragement."

DALE CARNEGIE TODAY

Carnegie's teachings are as fresh and inspiring now as on the day he assembled them in the mid-1930s. If he was bigger than life while alive, it may be said that in death he has become an institution,

action PLAN

1 Rise to the challenge. Growth comes from testing yourself and taking risks. Dale Carnegie jumped from one new challenge to the next, willing to risk failure for a chance at success. How can you look for new challenges and learn to face them more eagerly?

2 Take an interest in others. Carnegie earned praise as a "fascinating conversationalist" – just by listening attentively. Effective customer service starts with salespeople who want to know more about their customers professionally and personally. What can you do to learn more about your buyers and show them you care?

3 Keep it simple. Simple, straightforward language makes your message easy to understand. Carnegie used "simple language to reinforce universal principles" – and spoke with greater impact as a result. How can you use terms to show knowledge of your industry, yet keep your message simple?

with tenfold growth in 30 years. There are two reasons for the continued success of Dale Carnegie. One is the universal appeal of the teachings, which have been expanded to include courses in management training and sales training. The other is the concept of stewardship which Carnegie's successors put to work within the organization soon after his death.

It's an inspiring story, one J. Oliver Crom relishes telling: "Shortly after Mr. Carnegie died, a group of businesspeople came to Mrs. Carnegie and said, 'We're here to purchase the company – this is what we're offering and you'd better take it.' She turned them down.

"The following June at our convention, Dorothy Carnegie rose before the assembly and said, 'This is a sad time for all of us, following my husband's death. I don't know what you all are planning to do, but I know what I'm planning to do.'

"Talk about inspiration. Everyone wanted to know what they could do to help. And that's when this organization began to take on truly national proportions," says Crom.

fascinating fact

Dale Carnegie once purchased 180-million-year-old dinosaur tracks from the Peabody Museum of Yale University.

Under Dorothy Carnegie's direction, the company introduced stronger, more centralized management and financial planning. It formalized instructor training programs to ensure the highest-quality hired marketing specialists, and launched its first national advertising campaign.

All of this was accomplished in the space of one year – 1957. Today, as Dale Carnegie & Associates nears the 50th anniversary of *How to Win Friends and Influence People*, it can look with pride on having trained 3,000 instructors offering courses in 1,000 cities. Graduates now number more than three million people, compared to 350,000 at the time of Dale Carnegie's death.

Crom attributes this success to Dorothy Carnegie, who ran the company for 20 years. Now Crom himself is the steward, and as he considers the growth of the organization he muses on the "problems" that sometimes attend success.

"Our image is so good in the area of public speaking that many people don't realize we also have the other programs to satisfy very special needs within an organization," says Crom.

Dale Carnegie is alive and well. ▣

Good selling is more about caring than closing. Prospects "buy" you as well as your product — making them feel important makes you hard to resist. With Dale Carnegie's persistence, interest in others and desire to serve, your success odds improve. To get your people skills up to par, take this benchmark quiz to reveal your strengths and weaknesses.

⑤**=Always,** ④**=Often,** ③**=Sometimes,** ②**=Rarely,** ①**=Never**

1. I pursue challenging prospects in spite of the possibility of failure.

   ⑤   ④   ③   ②   ①

2. I make a point of asking buyers about their families and hobbies, and remember the information they share.

   ⑤   ④   ③   ②   ①

3. Instead of trying to impress prospects with "10-cent" words, I keep my language clear and simple.

   ⑤   ④   ③   ②   ①

4. I can make a presentation without letting fear sabotage my performance.

   ⑤   ④   ③   ②   ①

5. On every call, I make my buyer feel important and appreciated.

   ⑤   ④   ③   ②   ①

6. I treat big and small customers with the courtesy and respect they deserve.

   ⑤   ④   ③   ②   ①

Your Total _____

Your Final Score: Add your score for each question to get your final score. If you scored:

From 25 to 30 points: You make everyone feel like a million! Keep your selling skills as polished as your relationship skills, and your success is ensured.

From 18 to 24 points: Fear and/or greed may be holding you back. Learn to view challenges as opportunities, and customers as individuals with real emotions who want to feel valued and valuable. On every call, pay your buyer a sincere compliment or ask about a nonbusiness issue that's of particular interest to them.

Below 18 points: Why so cold? If your customers feel no personal connection to you, another vendor might easily lure them away. Put *How to Win Friends and Influence People* at the top of your reading list, and translate its lessons into specific action steps to use with your prospects and customers.

ALL KIDDING ASIDE, COMEDIAN JOHN CLEESE

HELPS YOU USE ACTING SKILLS FOR BETTER

MANAGEMENT AND PRESENTATIONS THAT

ALWAYS GET A CURTAIN CALL.

PHOTO BY O'SULLIVAN-SPOONER/GAMMA LIAISON

John Cleese

I n a perfect world, a friendly gesture is just what it seems. In the real world what a prospect expresses nonverbally may not match the words he or she is using. In the following *Selling Power* exclusive conversation with actor, writer, director/producer, creative genius John Cleese, readers are treated to a rare glimpse of this talented British wit.

Although Cleese is best known for such highly successful comic escapades as *Monty Python's Flying Circus, Fawlty Towers* and *A Fish Called Wanda*, he has made an equal success in the business world. In fact, Video Arts, the training film company that he co-founded in 1972, was purchased by management for 50 million British pounds. This versatile superstar has a rare ability to apply his multifaceted talents to practical pursuits. He has created wealth by teaching us how to laugh at ourselves. With his guffaws on hold and his keen sense of the human spirit at work, Cleese models some of the poses prospects strike while trying to avoid making the decision to buy. John Cleese may have gotten his first instinctive lessons in the art of persuasion from his father, who sold insurance.

fascinating fact

After its first season in America, Monty Python's Flying Circus *was picked up by 64 stations and became the highest-rated series in public television history.*

Cleese views his early years as traditional and, as he says, rather uneventful. Although his parents were loving and attentive, they were also typically reserved and even inhibited. His father, who spent a great deal of time traveling around the Gloucester countryside to see clients, did impart certain basics to young Cleese.

"I got the impression from him that there was a lot of psychology to selling. Sometimes, to tease potential customers who had been a little bit rude or insensitive or something like that, he had very subtle ways to confuse them. I can remember driving down a narrow country lane once and a car came screaming around the corner – very much on the wrong side of the road – it came screaming to a halt. To our astonishment (my mother was in the car too), the guy leapt out at us and started shouting all sorts of abuses and accusations at my father, who was a very careful, orderly driver. When he finished, there was some silence. My father looked at him and with a big smile said, 'Ah, I see you are a fine old English gentleman.' The guy's expression absolutely changed. He stared at my father for about 15 seconds and then said, 'As a matter of fact, I am, yes!' And then he got back in his car and drove off. It was an absolutely inspired thing my father said. When customers gave my father a difficult time, he could deflect their difficult behavior in much the same way."

> ## fascinating fact
>
> *Over a four-year period, Cleese's* The Life of Brian *grossed $75 million.*

FISHING FOR CRITICISM

Cleese once described himself as a gawky, very uncomfortable teenager, especially when he started growing so tall (he is six foot five). When he realized that he had a unique way of using his body – a way that was funny to people – he began to develop a presence around that skill. He began to feel self-confident enough to make presentations to fellow students and friends. Much later in life, Cleese formed his own company to use some of those same skills to train business professionals.

"The only way that you can develop your own presence is to get out and do it. And then try to get people to give you honest criticism. I'm not particularly keen for my daughter, who wants to be an actress, to go to drama school. I would much rather that she started to work in something and then start to take some specific courses. I believe you can learn about audiences by getting out there in front of them. And it's absolutely essential afterward to get feedback.

"You know I think people don't understand what rehearsal is. Rehearsal is actually getting up there and doing it and discovering that at this point you constantly misread this particular line. And then you have to have feedback. And it's difficult to get feedback."

To get that essential feedback, Cleese has developed questioning techniques that reveal more than a simple "Oh, I liked it just fine." In his structured and precise method, he has created a way for his critics to help him build a better mousetrap.

"You have to ask people in a crafty way. I organized a charity show in London two weeks ago and I did a piece of a sketch which I thought was very funny. I showed it to all the people who were helping me put the show together and they all said they thought it was funny. But I could sense that they weren't deep down comfortable about it. And I said, 'I don't think you think it's good.' And they said, 'No, no, yeah, I think it's fine. It's OK.' But I knew, although no one said anything negative about it, that it wasn't good enough and so I cut it.

"You see, they don't want to hurt your feelings. So it's very hard to get feedback. The way you ask for the criticism is very important. If you want to hear that it was fine, you will hear that it was fine. I'd have a question like, 'If I were shooting this movie again, what two things would you advise me to change?' And somehow then it becomes a positive act...a helpful act rather than a criticism."

BE YOURSELF – BUT BETTER

Many salespeople feel that if you look good – look like you're in control – you're going to be successful. Some cast themselves with motivational techniques to fend off the feelings of inadequacy that often accompany selling rejections. Cleese relates that to a theatrical performance and how an actor first develops the role.

"I immediately think of some actors who work inside out and some work outside in. The British tend to work outside in and the Americans work from inside out. And I can somehow just imagine all of these salespeople sort of coating themselves because they're scared and they want a kind of armor. In the beginning of my career I had a good act and you get to know how to carry the act off. And you can run into trouble if you get too spontaneous, too loose during a performance. And then if you've got to act just to get along, it becomes more and more obvious.

"I think also that as you get older, you get a bit more comfortable with yourself and then your own presence. You just say, 'Well, this is who I am. It's not perfect, but it's fine.' In my case I think it's come from analysis. The more you know about yourself, the more you accept yourself.

"Anyone who is doing cold calling has got to have some sort of personality to present to the people that he calls on. It's just too tough to go in naked. And, at the same time, the more they use that, the more it's going to repel. My opinion is you certainly have to rehearse. You have to regard a presentation to people as a bit of a performance. But at the same time when you're writing it, try to write it in your own language. Say it the way that you would want to say it yourself and try to perform it in as natural a way as possible."

Director Cleese has coached many talented performers in structuring a particular bit or character. On when and how to drop the rehearsal text and improvise he is, as ever, practical.

On sales calls, your image may persuade as much as high quality or great value. To cultivate the confidence and self-assurance that turns prospects to buyers, Cleese suggests developing your own presence. Be comfortable with yourself and rehearse your delivery. When your image packs a punch, your words carry more weight.

Present with presence. Presence helps you get your buyers' attention during presentations and helps them remember you later. "The only way that you can develop your own presence is to get out and do it," says Cleese. "And then try to get people to give you honest criticism." Let your personality shine through in your presentations to let buyers know you're one of a kind.

achieuement LESSONS

Learn to like yourself. You don't have to be perfect to be happy with yourself. Cleese says that the better you know yourself, the more you accept yourself. Look inward to find out what makes you tick, then think about how to turn your unique qualities into selling advantages.

Rehearse to get it right. "You have to regard a presentation to people as a bit of a performance," says Cleese. "But at the same time, try to perform it in as natural a way as possible." Practice helps you learn your presentation and get comfortable with it so you look and feel more confident.

"It's a question of personality. I mean some people can improvise and it's marvelous if you can do it. But I think most people can't. I would always try to structure it as much as possible. Unfortunately a lot of people who think they have a facility for talking are simply people who talk too much.

"If you want to maintain composure under pressure, I recommend that you don't fiddle. Try to keep your hands still. Move as little as you possibly can because it looks better. If you're going to make a gesture, make it an easy, fairly big one. Try it in front of the mirror. Don't make short, small, jerky, restrictive movements.

"But the final thing that we keep coming back to, which is so fascinating and so difficult, is how do you become better and more spontaneous? Through practice...and the rest comes down to your self-confidence. Are you getting to know more about yourself? It is not necessary to present this rather tough, invulnerable facade. It's a tremendous help, and also very appealing to people, to sometimes say, 'I just don't know, I'm really not sure about it.'"

A WINNING TEAM

On such complex long-range projects as the movie *A Fish Called Wanda*, external forces are always present pulling at the creative person's focus. It's much the same when a salesperson is trying to sell to a committee or land a large corporate customer. The world seems to conspire to put roadblocks in the path – obstacles that can pull you off and make you forget your way.

"I was executive producer on *Wanda*. I was almost the CEO on it. I set the thing up, helped raise the money, chose the crew, supervised the script, sat in on the editing, was in on the viewings, did the publicity. I was in on almost every aspect of it.

"I accomplished all my goals mainly by having excellent people out there. In the early stages it was not difficult. Getting the script together was very simple, working with Charlie [Charles Chrichton, co-author with Cleese of the original Wanda story] and then Jamie and Kevin [co-stars Jamie Lee Curtis and Kevin Kline] to get the script out. I was able to supervise that and once we got the script out, then it was the job of raising the money and

action PLAN

1 Get more out of every sale. For Cleese, learning and personal relationships make acting rewarding. For you, serving customers, professional growth or some other goal may be the driving force. How can you make selling more rewarding and motivating to maintain your success?

2 Know your buyer better. To draw a great performance out of an actor or information from a prospect, make that person feel secure. How can you improve your questioning strategy to make buyers open up to you?

3 Have a plan. When making *A Fish Called Wanda*, Cleese knew planning ahead of time could eliminate mistakes later. How can you learn more about your buyers and predict their objections before you call on them?

4 Get a second opinion. When others didn't like a routine he thought was funny, Cleese scrapped it. To improve your presentations get feedback from another person. What questions can you ask to get constructive criticism of your performance?

putting the team together, choosing the crew.

"When we started to shoot, that was when I started saying, 'You do this,' and 'You do this.' I supervised the schedule because I wanted to make sure that we had the right amount of time, the right number of days for each scene, because that's something I feel very strongly about."

Cleese laid conscious, careful plans for the writing and filming. He wanted to make it a success. "Yes, I thought about it inasmuch as I made sure that there was an enormous amount of time up front for all the planning. I think most movies go wrong because they start before the script is ready. I was working on the script with the actors concerned nearly 20 months before the cameras started to roll. I mean I sat with Jamie in a Los Angeles restaurant and talked with her 20 months before she started to shoot. So at the time that she rehearsed, which was after 19 months, she knew what the character was – she was discovering new stuff but not the basic character. And we had that kind of cooperation."

It's the pre-planning management that makes the difference, whether it's on a movie lot, in a corporate boardroom, or in the field selling. "Yes, tremendous planning. So everybody has masses of time to ask all kinds of questions that they have to ask about this scene or that scene...what's this about...why's he doing this? And then the really difficult scenes we discussed several times. We talked about why he says that or makes this move. So everybody gets a clearer understanding of what's going to happen. And that's just a function of time. Everybody's door is open because everybody has time for everybody else."

Like any good manager, Cleese recognizes the

importance of getting a positive group consensus before making final decisions. Getting the team to play from the same game card, getting them to know their individual parts and where they fit into the whole and letting them express individual concerns and needs. And then he knows when to cut the cord, come to grips with the final effort, make the play and score. "It's very much orchestrated. And every person was important and they knew they were valued which is very important. And they also communicated with each other. They didn't always have to go through the conductor, unless they needed a conductor."

BONDING WITH BUYERS

Cleese knows how to get that special performance out of an actor. A great performance is not something that automatically happens. It's a subtle combination of acting skill and the director's expertise at drawing it out.

"You have to get the feeling of each person – that you really understand where they are coming from. In other words, for each person to say, 'Now do I have some sort of picture in my mind about this person and the job that he's doing?' You know people often say to me, 'Gosh, you're asking a lot of questions,' and I'm thinking, 'Well do I?' I mean all I'm doing is trying to understand. And therefore I'm asking questions. I go on until basically I understand and there comes a moment when I say, 'Yeah, all right, I don't have all the details but I have the overall picture and I can fill in the details later.' And I think that's the beginning.

"If you sit down with someone, you have to make them feel as secure as possible because the more secure they feel with you, the more they feel that you're accepting them, the more they will give you the unbiased truth and the more you can then discuss how to solve the problem. The less secure they feel, the more they will try to conceal their problems. So the harder it will be for you to find out what they really need and how you can help them, what they need to work on. Whereas the English are far too indirect, in my observa-

fascinating fact

Cleese has made commercials for Asiaweek *magazine in Hong Kong, peanut butter cups in Canada and fish fingers in Australia.*

tion, Americans are often very aggressive in their business behavior – in a way that I think is counterproductive. They may want to be tough. They may want to look like sort of tight-lipped, granite men."

In Cleese's view, managers who subscribe to the Rambo management school accomplish less than their more intuitive, sensitive counterparts. For certain types of salespeople, he also recognizes the value of a stronger hand with a shove in the right direction. A sales manager, it seems, must be all things to all salespeople.

"Of course, if you behave like Rambo, everyone's going to behave back to you like that. I think you have to give people the security of knowing that you value them and basically that they're a valued member of the team. That if they are therefore valued, they will be valuable.

"Now it's harder if you inherit the team. And it would be difficult to manage someone that you don't think is very good. But I still think that the way to make progress with him or her is ultimately to talk it through and not to do this Rambo management type of thing which is to try to make yourself feel good by making the other person feel bad. Also maybe by trying to find out what is good in that person even though you may not respond to that person immediately. To recognize that everybody has some potential. Say, 'All right, is he as bad as I think?' I mean I find it very difficult sometimes to assess the people."

THE FIRE INSIDE

Cleese, whose career began when he was hired fresh out of Oxford University to write comedy for BBC Radio, is not motivated by traditional show business values. Adulation of fans is not what brings peace to his soul. Although he has made a fantastic financial success, money is not his primary goal.

"I think sometimes you find something deeply satisfying because you basically got it right. And that happens sometimes as with the scripts for *Fawlty Towers*, the movie *Life of Brian*, a television Shakespeare production, and of course *Wanda*. For me personally, the thing that gives me the most satisfaction is the sense that I've understood something which I never understood before. When I work with people, if I don't feel like I'm learning, I get very bored."

Finding meaning in that daily grind is a challenge for all of us. We tend to think of the glamour of show business and we forget all the repeated rehearsals, failed shows, repetitive performances and dark, dusty dressing rooms where none of the thrill of cheering crowds greets the veteran performer. Professionals can't say, "Well, I've had enough of this" and walk off the set, any more than a salesperson can walk out of a prospect's office when the going gets tough.

"I'm not talking as a trainer but I think meaning has to come out of the personal relationships you have with the people that you work with. Going on the floor to make my 81st training film is not something that sets the adrenaline pumping. But going on the floor and seeing all my old friends, enjoying working with them, that's what motivates me."

Any manager who has struggled to motivate a team of salespeople has pondered the problem of how to get each one going. You must be a coach to this one, a mentor to that one and a pest to the other. One is motivated by dreams of riches, another looks for the satisfaction in the job, and someone else likes dealing with the people. For Cleese, motivation is not a matter of cheering and singing company songs, but of commitment.

"You know, I don't think of it so much as building up a corporation. I don't think in those terms. To me, it has a lot more to do with the particular faces of the company. And a sense of commitment to them. I have the feeling that I will go on working with them because these people do this job well and they enjoy doing it and it's a good deal for everyone concerned. As far as the motivation, it has more to do with the idea that we're putting out ideas and training. This is a general culture which, in our own small way, may make slight improvements in the way people work.

"We think it's a much greater motivation to teach people skills that make them that much better at their jobs than to just give them a cheering session that will fade in a short time."

As a manager who has worked with businesspeople, a director who has worked with actors, a writer who has worked the production end of the business and a comedic genius who has enthralled audiences, Cleese is in a unique position to talk about what motivates people to give their best.

"My policy with people who work for me is always to be very supportive and encouraging and I'm told that this works very well with introverts. Whereas extroverts work much better if you cheer them along a bit. One of my friends, who is now a psychiatrist, was captain of an all-England cricket team and he was very, very successful and they had two very good fast fellas. And they used to treat them quite differently. Every time one guy would walk back before running out after the ball, they would say, 'Come on, let's go, that was great,' and that's how he got better. But the other guy, when he walked out they would be saying things like, 'What's the matter? You're walking like an old woman today. What's the matter with you?' Completely different treatments for both.

"I think really the key there is to get your own ego out of the way so that you can appreciate the qualities that you don't really have yourself. I mean I am an introvert and if I have to deal with an extrovert, I have to try to do it without letting my own tendencies get in the way."

For managers who have difficult situations to deal with, either within the sales team or with disgruntled customers, Cleese offers these words of advice.

"I would suggest to sit back – sort of take the pressure off – so he doesn't feel that he's being pursued and almost deliberately say, 'Can you talk a little bit about what's bothering you?' or 'It's very helpful to me, it may be helpful for our business, if I know what your problem is.' He may say, 'Oh, I don't like this, I don't like that.' Then you say, 'Can I ask you why?' Always ask them an open question.

"You see, if you are getting a difficult response, or if you can't make any sense out of the nonverbal cues you're getting, you just fiddle with the picture that you see in front of you. If you don't get it or you can't understand, try to find out. Don't put him under great pressure, ask open questions. Keep asking the open questions until you really understand him. It may be an objection that is actually nonexistent. It comes out of misunderstanding or something that you can fix and they didn't think you could fix it. Try to get a real picture of where they are. It means that you have to be open and relaxed yourself and not the driver or the pusher."

If you use humor to make a point, use it with caution. It can be a dangerous tool when applied with too much force or at the wrong time or in the wrong circumstances. It takes finesse to be able to wield a funny ax.

"I think it would be quite incorrect to use humor as a way of scoring a customer or making them feel smaller. I think you could laugh at almost anything except the customer." ▣

Benchmarking
YOUR SUCCESS

After years in show business, John Cleese knows what makes a convincing performance: Thorough planning, a well-rehearsed presentation and strong motivation, for starters. To incorporate these elements into your success strategy more consistently, take the quiz below. Your score will tell you if you need to clean up your act.

⑤=**Always,** ④=**Often,** ③=**Sometimes,** ②=**Rarely,** ①=**Never**

1. To constantly improve my presentation, I update it as needed based on criticism from others.

   ⑤   ④   ③   ②   ①

2. I plan every call in advance, taking into account the prospect's special needs.

   ⑤   ④   ③   ②   ①

3. I rehearse enough to deliver my presentation without struggling to remember key points or phrases.

   ⑤   ④   ③   ②   ①

4. I tailor my questioning strategy to my buyer's personality to encourage open communication.

   ⑤   ④   ③   ②   ①

5. I communicate openly with other members of my team to learn from them.

   ⑤   ④   ③   ②   ①

6. When dealing with others, I avoid "Rambo management" and treat people with sensitivity and respect.

   ⑤   ④   ③   ②   ①

Your Total _____

Your Final Score: Add your score for each question to get your final score. If you scored:

From 25 to 30 points: You know your lines and how to deliver them. Guard against the complacency success often brings and continue to fine-tune your presentation and your performance.

From 18 to 24 points: Due to lack of preparation or confidence, perhaps, open communication sometimes unsettles you. Strive to know yourself and your message well instead of expecting perfection in either. Don't be afraid to make mistakes — just be sure to learn from them.

Below 18 points: Your presentation and interpersonal skills need polish. Have your manager go over the elements of effective presentations with you, then design a presentation for one of your prospects and rehearse it for an audience. Tell yourself, "I have a message my buyers need to hear."

MICHAEL DELL LETS CUSTOMERS HAVE IT THEIR

WAY. ADOPT HIS ENERGY, COMPETITIVE

SPIRIT AND COMMITMENT TO CUSTOMER

SATISFACTION AND YOU, TOO, CAN BE LIKE MIKE.

PHOTO BY KALUZNY/GAMMA LIAISON

michael Dell

After all these years they still don't take young Michael Dell seriously – and he seems to like it that way. Although press reports about his childhood business acumen are contradictory, they go something like this. At seven little Michael was ready to make his first big move. According to one story he tried to enroll in a correspondence school to get a college diploma. Another account has him taking mail order courses for his high school diploma. One thing is sure. He was in a hurry to get somewhere.

Press reports say that at 12 (some say 13) Michael earned $2,000 selling stamps on consignment out of a rented post office box. Still other stories have him starting a mail order stamp-trading business by publishing his own list of stamps and auctioning them off. At 15 (or some say 16) he bought up lists of newlyweds from Town Hall, called them up to offer a newspaper subscription and supposedly broke sales records at the *Houston Post*. Other reports say he recruited high school buddies a year later to do the same over the phone netting Michael a cool $18,000 (or some say $17,000) which he then invested in a brand-new BMW.

Michael Dell told *Selling Power*: "In most counties in Texas, when you get married you have to register at the county courthouse. I had the idea of sending a direct mail offer to these addresses. I got this idea because I was selling subscriptions on the phone and people buying were often newlyweds. The other group that I found bought a paper most often had just moved to a new house. So I got lists from banks of people who had just gotten a new mortgage." Even as a teenag-

> ## fascinating fact
>
> *Dell hid his IBM PCs in his dorm roommate's bathtub when his parents visited him at the University of Texas.*

31

er, Dell instinctively saw the hidden power of using solid prospect lists and the telephone to close sales.

Whether any of these accounts is the absolute, whole truth we'll never know. By now the factual stories are likely forever buried in Dell Computer Corp.'s instant nostalgia file. Yet one fact remains. At 27 Michael Dell owns 30 percent of a company that currently does over $12 billion in sales worldwide.

fascinating fact

Dell's dorm room business officially became Dell Computer Corporation on May 3, 1984.

In the computer field even upstarts have no business turning the billion dollar corner until they are at least 25. But this legendary dorm room computer entrepreneur seems to have eclipsed even Steve Jobs' 20th century American started-in-a-garage success story. And it's not over yet.

With sales figures climbing above $12 billion and competitors running for cover, Michael Dell has all but declared war on the way computers have always been sold and serviced. In fact, some industry pundits believe that Dell has fueled a raging fire that will consume every also-ran in the business leaving the computer consumer at a banquet with only four plates left on the table – IBM, Compaq, Dell and Apple. Other management gurus claim that Dell has nowhere to go but, eventually, down. Nervous computer and peripheral dealers are looking over their collective shoulder to see whose neck will feel the ax next while rival PC clone Compaq has dropped prices so fast would-be buyers have hardly been able to rewrite their checks.

To make the computer market even more itchy, on the day *SP* was to interview Michael Dell, remarks by a Wall Street analyst at Kidder Peabody that Dell Computer Corp. had accounted improperly for foreign currency trades sent Dell stock sliding nearly 10 percent. With Dell one of the hottest stocks around, the rumor sent paroxysms through Dell Computer Corp.'s headquarters in Austin. Managers scurried, spokespersons grabbed for phones, legal arms stretched across the country. By day's end, the Wall Street analyst had suffered a slapped wrist, Dell had solidified its backing in the financial community, the foreign currency flap had been clarified and Michael Dell had emerged – once again – the winner!

You don't have to be Sherlock Holmes to find evidence of Michael Dell's customer commitment. When you tell buyers you value them, let your actions back you up. Act on Dell's advice to make great service a practice — not just a policy.

Build the organization around the customer. With computers customized to buyer needs, toll-free support and a nationwide network of service providers, Dell is truly customer-driven. To win more buyers, make it easy for them to buy and own your product. Streamline sales and service procedures to make buying, asking questions and solving problems fast and easy.

achievement
LESSONS

Offer more quality for less money. Dell modified IBMs to offer buyers more power and speed for less money. To lower your price or add value to sales, consider what you offer customers now and what you could offer if you worked a little harder or settled for a slightly smaller commission. Survey buyers to find out what they value and seek out ways to provide it at less cost.

Use feedback to improve. With records of order and support calls, Dell can research problems and design permanent solutions. To keep the customers you worked hard to earn, make their opinions count. When they offer suggestions or criticism, use the feedback to correct the cause of problems and make lasting improvements.

THE BEST TARGET TO SHOOT AT

To those who have watched Dell's rise from college hacker to corporate tycoon in just shy of nine years, this comes as no surprise. For Michael Dell is a fierce competitor. Willing to take on the biggest guns in the fleet, he sails into harm's way with nothing more than a sleek plan to outfox even the most entrenched armada.

What's his secret? Well, that competitive spirit doesn't hurt. Add to that the crystal clear thinking of a visionary, the keen sense of what the market wants, a willingness to learn what he doesn't yet know and the desire to surround himself with the brightest minds to handle specific tasks and you have one entrepreneur who is redefining the way America, and the world, buys computers. But there is just one more thing. Michael Dell is a brilliant salesman.

Taken as individual units, none of these qualities would add up to the success story folks are spreading about Dell.

Is he a genius? Well, not technically. That is, he didn't come up with any

action PLAN

1 Innovate! Original ideas help you stand out from the competition. "We always look for ways to change things and make things better," says Dell. How can you improve products, speed up delivery and response to customers and make your performance stronger than ever?

2 Set goals. Dell believes in setting objectives that "stretch goals for building the organization." To improve with every quarter, keep challenging yourself. What goals can you set for different areas of performance and how can you develop strategies to meet them?

3 Learn from mistakes. To reach your potential, risk and mistakes are inevitable. Dell says he "learned by what worked — by trial and error," and so should you. How can you step outside your comfort zone more often, and find the lessons in the mistakes you make as a result?

technological breakthrough. He's no Jobs or Wozniak. Did he sell out his year's quota at IBM in one month and then sit around looking for something else to do? Well, not exactly. He never worked for anyone else. So, he's no Ross Perot.

Has he taken the systems that other people developed, looked at them in a fresh way, analyzed what the customer wants, cut margins, streamlined production, cut out the middleman and turned telemarketing into an art form? Yes, that's closer. Dell may be a new-age industrial cousin to Henry Ford. What Ford did for the assembly line, Dell has done for the marketing line. Dell's delivery systems also may be the logical offshoot of Fred Smith's predictable overnight service at Federal Express.

Let's take a look at Dell's theory and how he put it into practice. One: Retail stores are not the best places to buy computers. Why? Because most of the people who work there know little about the computers they are selling. In many cases they know even less than the buyers.

Two: Retail stores charge more for the added value that they rarely give the customer.

Three: Retail stores sell end users off-the-shelf products that may or may not suit their needs.

So here are lessons one, two, and three from Michael Dell on how to build a billion-dollar business selling computers.

"First," he told *SP*, "build the organization around the customer. When you look at this business, it's been one of customer responsiveness and being able to satisfy the customer. Second, create a spirit of innovation within the business. We always look for ways to change things and ways to make things better. Customer responsiveness, innovation and change and ongoing improvement. Third, set objectives that stretch goals for building the organization."

That sounds simple enough. Dell goes on to describe the initial stages of his computer sales revolution.

"The idea in my mind was that selling personal computers and related equipment through the dealer was very inefficient and the service was very poor. If you could sell the part directly through to the end user and talk directly to the end user you would have better support, more efficiency and a happier customer and you would have a great business," he explained.

That was in the beginning, way back in, oh, let's see, '83/'84 when Dell Computer Corporation was doing business out of Michael Dell's University of Texas dorm room under the name PC's Limited. Dell, who had taken to hanging out in computer stores during his high school years, one day went home and ripped the guts out of his Apple to see what made it tick. Now a college man, Mr. Dell began buying up surplus parts – disk drives and the like – from local dealers with an excess of inventory they were only too happy to unload on the bespectacled kid with a dream. (He wore thick glasses then – today he sports contact lenses and $600 suits.) Little did the dealers know he'd one day be cutting them right out of the picture. Color me outdated and overpriced.

A BRILLIANT NEW MARKETING PLAN

With the parts, Dell began to assemble – and sell – his first PC clones. By souping up stripped-down IBM machines, he could produce more speed and power at a fraction of the cost. He sold the first units to friends on campus and word of mouth spread. He became a man with a mission.

And what about Mom and Dad, and the tuition they had shelled out? Well, Mom's a stockbroker who understands the value of solid sales and Dad's an orthodontist who, by the way, showed up at Sonny's dorm unexpectedly one day and caught Michael and his cronies in mid-business transaction. It was time for a talk. The armistice they worked out looked like this:

At the end of his first college year – May 1984 – Michael would take his profits – $20,000 – and set up shop in an Austin storefront. If by the end of August things did not look bright and promising, the three Dells would redeal and Michael would return to his premed studies.

Dell shifted into second to begin the long uphill climb. He offered custom-built computers to doctors, lawyers and small businesses, always getting half the money up front to buy components. These cash, credit card or check deals kept Dell's cash flow healthy.

In the first month Dell and his minions sold $180,000 worth of computer hardware. By plowing every cent back into inventory and salaries, after nine months sales had soared to $6 million. By the beginning of 1985, Dell was employing 39 people and set to launch a national advertising campaign to attract small- and medium-size PC users.

fascinating fact

In 1994 Dell introduced the Latitude – the first notebook computer with coast-to-coast battery life.

IT'S WAR!

The ads offered an 800 number service to order customized machines, a concept that the big guns in the business were too slow witted to grab. Users could select speed, memory, drives and other peripherals. Since they were buying direct from the manufacturer (Dell was still assembling parts that he bought all over the place; as every hacker knew, they were, in fact, the same parts everyone else in the business was using), customers got more performance for a much lower cost – up to 30 percent. What's not to like?

Well, for starters, customers didn't want to have to lose their newer, faster, souped-up machines for two or three or more days when they needed service. Since Dell was an over-the-phone-we'll-ship-it-out-right-away-and-if-anything-goes-wrong-you-ship-it-back-and-we'll-fix-it-and-then-ship-it-back-to-you shop, customers were getting a little hot under the keyboard.

To fix the problem, Dell made a service deal with a national company that already had a computer repair force all over America and, almost overnight, these techies were appearing at Dell customer sites to repair or replace broken boxes. In March 1989, Dell made the same deal with Xerox Corporation which took over the Dell repair contract.

Dell also set up a toll-free customer support service which today registers calls in the tens of thousands. Such calls also serve to keep Dell aware of just where the market's heading and what it's hot for. By keeping records of all the order and support calls in a database, Dell engineers can call up anyone's record instantaneously, offer a temporary solution, and then move right over to R & D to research the problem and come up with a permanent solution or new component. But we're getting ahead of our story. That's the way it is with Dell. Things always seem to move faster than you expect.

Take the critics. Dell told *SP*, "Early on, the company was always winning the editor's choice awards." Take advertising: "I can remember the first ad that we did. An ad guy literally sketched it out on the back of a pizza box. We just learned by what worked – by trial and error." The ads that followed took direct aim at industry leaders IBM and Compaq. Again, that competitive drive. Take service: Dell has established an unbeatable reputation by being ranked number one for customer satisfaction by the J.D. Power & Associates survey of small- and medium-size businesses.

Well, OK, here we've got a whiz kid who's not quite out of the whiz mold. He's not just a techie, not just a businessman, not just a salesman, not just a fierce competitor. So what is he and what exactly does he do that's breaking all the growth and sales records across the computer industry?

To sum it all up, he's a margin cutter. He's cutting production margins, price margins, delivery margins, service margins, research and development margins, sales margins and even time margins. He's found a way to look at literally every function within his company and industry and cut the time it takes to perform it. As he said in an interview way back in 1987, "I'm fascinated with the idea of eliminating unnecessary steps."

PRICE ALONE WON'T CUT IT

And that's what rival companies failed to realize about the Dell phenomenon. Dell is not just taking orders by mail and cutting out the dealer. He has concepted an entire new way to approach a market, discover what it wants and then respond to its demands quickly and effectively. He has invented and trained his sales and service army to use the marketing equivalent of a high-tech Gatling gun. He even has a name for it – direct relationship marketing.

This year Dell stock appreciated more than 200 percent for the second consecutive year. So competitive is this boy brain trooper, that at one company party Dell showed up in army fatigues signaling no let up in the combative stance he has always promoted toward the competition. And this after the company won every bout in a knockout. It's good to be king! It's better to keep your forces on the alert for the next salvo.

Maintaining high growth and profit at the same time takes, in Michael Dell's own words, "a balance between the growth activities and building of a structure to support those. They have to be in concert because when one gets ahead of the other there is trouble.

"What we did is actually build our team based on our capabilities. We had pretty well agreed to standards of performance and things that we would watch and identify. We carefully watched if we were not executing the business in a way that was correct. Today, obviously in a business like ours, inventories are watched very carefully, the margins, our expenses are watched very carefully, there is a very good understanding throughout the ranks of what the parameters are of success.

"I think you must constantly have well-established and well-agreed-to goals, especially when you are operating in a crazy environment, because you don't necessarily have the time to sit down and have long meetings and develop strategies. But if everyone knows what the targets are, then you have a better chance of hitting some of them. My role now is to set the direction for the business. What markets should we expand to, what strategies should we pursue, what are the objectives we should have for our business?"

AGGRESSIVE AND COMPETITIVE

Michael Dell has managed to weather stormy seas and chart a clear course to the future by relying on some very sage advice: "My father used to say, 'Play nice, but win.' Basically the idea is that there a lot of people out there who don't necessarily play fair, but use tricks, or don't use the highest ethical standards.

"One of the things that is important when you have a very aggressive company, and a very aggressive strategy, you have to have very clearly established guidelines of what is acceptable and what is not. Sometimes in the pursuit of winning some people cross the line of what is acceptable, so it is very important to have clear, ethical guidelines for the company. So that someone does not do what he thought was the right thing for the company, but was wrong, or harmful or not legal." (Dell Computer Corp. also has written guidelines that employees sign.)

"I think healthy competition is more than winning. Healthy competition is when all players in the same market are playing by the same rules."

> **fascinating fact**
>
> *As of August 1998, Dell employed 20,800 employees worldwide.*

To become a successful salesperson, Dell stresses "...understanding the needs of the other person, and the ability of communicating the value of what you have to offer. Motivation plays a key role. In a business like ours, where there is ongoing growth and a lot of opportunities, it is easy to get excited by the success of the business. At the same time we have to leverage that excitement and energy toward the process of continuing that success. The key is to provide an environment that allows for growth and convincing our people that they can indeed achieve great, great things. Giving them the tools they need and having parameters for setting goals that are very aggressive."

AN AMAZING CORPORATE CULTURE

Michael Dell once said that he wanted to grow at outrageous rates and do amazing things. "We are pretty much on track," he told *SP*. "Obviously we can't grow at a 150 percent rate all the time. But this year many things happened, a whole series of things, the international expansion, the growth of our channels, our growth rate in mature markets, our ability to expand our internal cost structure. By 1987 or 1988 we realized that by 1992 we could do a billion." As everyone now knows, Dell hopped over that mark to make it an even $2 billion.

Corporate culture at Dell is clearly defined. Says Michael, "It's very simple. Responsive, customer focused, high intensity level." How does Michael Dell handle rejection? "You stand up and fight back." To recover after a disappointment, "Get back and fight harder." How has Michael Dell handled the shift from teenage tycoon to mature CEO? "There are a number of issues you have to deal with as a CEO that don't directly relate to the business of producing and selling products. That's stuff you have to learn. My philosophy is to have all the advice I can get from the most talented people I can find. I think you have to be confident, not arrogant. There is a big difference between confidence and arrogance. Confidence is belief in your abilities, and arrogance is disregarding reality."

Being on the inside of Dell Computer Corp. is similar to residing in the brain of Michael Dell. "One thing I will tell you," says Dell of the company he has nurtured, "inside the company we are very self-critical. Especially within the top 100 managers in the company. We are very frank and very open about our problems in the company. And we are quite objective in the pursuit of an answer and I think that this is extremely helpful. You need to ensure that active and objective discussions are going on."

fascinating fact

In September 1997, Dell's incoming call rate reached almost 1,700 per day.

For Dell moving forward is a process. "I try to get people to think about the process that I go through to come up with ideas instead of just saying, 'Here is an idea.' For example, when we were talking with CompUSA, a software house, I came in one day and said to someone, 'We should be working with them. Go look at it and see what you think.' And gradually he saw the learning process I would go through. I think you can teach people to be more innovative. Because we accept change and innovation, and people are encouraged to argue, we have incredibly inventive and creative people, and that's very positive."

At Dell Computer it's not unusual to see signs that exhort you to take a risk. "The message is for everybody," explains Dell. "Everybody is supposed to think about risk. The problem is not my taking a risk, the problem is that as the company grows, you want people to continue to take risks and be inventive and to think about ongoing improvement."

GOING GLOBAL

What about the future for Dell Computer? "I think that the information technology business is going to undergo huge restructuring from a technological standpoint, in the products that follow from that, in the ways that products are sold and the companies that sell them," Dell told *SP*. "I believe that the traditional companies like IBM or DEC are going to be faced with a mammoth restructuring. That provides great opportunity for some fast and flexible companies that can provide the products and services required. They have an exceptional opportunity for the next few years.

"To cash in on these opportunities," Dell went on, "we'll be building a global distribution system and relationships with our customers. I think it is having the production capability required to deliver those products to the customer, and growing the services we provide, and not just providing a box, but providing a complete computer or complete networks of computers and services and support that go around those computers. So, in essence, we will be delivering total solutions as they relate to all parts."

In fact, Dell has already made significant inroads internationally. After entering the European market in 1988 with zero sales, by February 3, 1992, Dell was doing $240 million. European sales constituted 30 percent of Dell's total sales.

"We opened up directly into about 20 countries and we have distributors in 50 other countries. We are running at about one country a month in terms of direct distribution and in the last quarter in every country we grew over 125 percent including the U.K., Germany, France and Canada," Dell told *SP*. How does he reproduce his American success – over there? "I think you don't necessarily transplant it," said Dell. "You take an idea or a concept and then you mold it to the specific market. Get talented people from the particular market that you are entering to execute that concept and then you leave them alone and let them do their thing. For example, if you look at our business in Germany there is a much higher content of eye-to-eye selling with large accounts, than there is in the U.S. That is really a top requirement.

"I think cultures are very different and there is no such thing as the correct way of doing business all over the world. It has to be a molded image in each market, but it should be equally positive and easy to any customer in any market. It's just going to be slightly different according to the environment. For example, we've got the best service and support in Czechoslovakia, but it is different from service and support in the U.S."

To be successful in foreign markets, Dell suggests building partnerships. "Basically, the idea is, get a bright person, an entrepreneur, or a businessperson who understands the computer industry and looks at the model, understands why these concepts and ideas apply to that specific marketplace and has qualified objectives. The primary objectives are to establish the direct selling model and have a high level of customer satisfaction. The financial objectives are really secondary, because if we reach the financial objective and not the customer relationship objectives, you get off to the wrong start. You start with getting the model in place and later on you reap the rewards."

> ## fascinating fact
>
> *Dell sales for the fiscal year ending February 2, 1997 totaled $7,759 million.*

Meet customer objectives and financial objectives will follow? Wall Street has to take a back seat to Main Street? What is this? Blasphemy?

"It's pretty obvious," Dell told *SP*. "Lots of companies have gone through a lot of problems and we've learned from them. I have done a lot of reading and I have a lot of curiosity. I've listened a lot." And after all the studying and reading and listening, Dell came back to basics. The customer is always right.

Dell is actively selling in western and eastern Europe, and the company already has plans to start up in China; and, according to Dell himself, he has traveled to Japan twice a year for the past seven or so years.

"Every time I go, I learn something," Dell said. "There is a respect for the customer that is very, very strong. It's the most interesting country in terms of contrasts. Japan is very precise. There is a great respect for excellence and a great respect for the future."

The same seems to be true at Dell Computer. And why not? Dell continues to stun his rivals and delight his customers. That seems to be an unbeatable combination. ▣

Even as a little tyke Michael Dell was big on competition, drive and vision. To be sure you're no stranger to success, make these and Dell's other important qualities part of your selling personality. Take the quiz below to measure how much of them you have and to learn hints on developing the ones you need.

⑤=Always, ④=Often, ③=Sometimes, ②=Rarely, ①=Never

1. Instead of doing what I've always done, I generate new ideas to help improve my performance.

   ⑤　　④　　③　　②　　①

2. I spend enough time prospecting with effective methods to keep my sales funnel full.

   ⑤　　④　　③　　②　　①

3. I enjoy competing with other salespeople and use competition to push myself to peak levels of performance.

   ⑤　　④　　③　　②　　①

4. When customers complain about a product or offer a suggestion, I act on their feedback.

   ⑤　　④　　③　　②　　①

5. Instead of letting mistakes get me down, I learn from them to prevent future errors.

   ⑤　　④　　③　　②　　①

6. When I can't make a sale ethically, I turn down the order.

   ⑤　　④　　③　　②　　①

Your Total _____

Your Final Score Add your score for each question to get your final score. If you scored:

From 25 to 30 points: You seem destined for Dell-like success. Keep a close eye on competitors and keep your selling skills polished and motivation high to stay ahead of them.

From 18 to 24 points: If you want to succeed, you have to get hungry. Good selling requires thought, but you must follow it up with action. Remind yourself of the rewards effort brings, and create itemized to-do lists that will help you do more every day.

Below 18 points: You seem stuck in neutral. To get back in gear, start using your head more often, and get closer to your customers to increase your desire to serve them. Get the training you need to correct any skill deficiencies, and put yourself on a daily diet of motivation to help you start thinking and acting more like a winner.

WITH TIME ON HIS SIDE, HUGH DOWNS

HELPS YOU CONQUER FEAR, REDUCE STRESS

AND THINK POSITIVELY TO LIVE AND

SELL BETTER AT ANY AGE.

PHOTO BY FINEMAN/SYGMA

Hugh Downs

The fluid, soft-spoken tones of Hugh Downs have entered our homes and our hearts for over 55 years. He has always raised the standards of excellence in his field. In an exclusive interview with *Selling Power*, 73-year-old Downs reveals the secrets behind his success in aging with grace, dignity and a zest for life. Most Americans probably recognize Hugh Downs as the Emmy award-winning host of the ABC newsmagazine *20/20* or the longtime emcee for the TV game show *Concentration*. Since hosting *Over Easy*, the 1975 PBS series on aging in America, Downs has become a well-respected educator on aging as he promotes awareness of issues affecting the over-50 generation. In his latest book, *Fifty To Forever*, Downs provides ample evidence that life's later years can be as productive and rewarding as any other time of life.

To back up this assertion, Downs cites a scientific study conducted by two Georgia researchers who tested 96 noninstitutionalized centenarians to discover the secret to long life. The researchers came up with an astonishing conclusion.

> ## fascinating fact
>
> *At age 22, Downs was America's youngest network announcer.*

POSITIVE ATTITUDE

"The common thread they found," Downs explains, "can be summed up in one word: attitude. These people tended to be optimistic, had found engagement or commitment to some interest, remained active and were able to adapt to loss. When I did a piece on the study for *20/20*, what really struck me was that they all took an amused but tolerant view of life. They might have been working for a cause, but they weren't zealous or hostile. They were doing what they could but still retaining some perspective and amusement about life."

Downs was also impressed by the fortitude the centenarians demonstrated when confronted with loss. The positive attitudes demonstrated by the study's subjects affirm the truism that an optimistic outlook produces not only a hap-

---

1. Start exercising. *The New England Journal of Medicine* reported on a study of about 10,000 Harvard graduates who were previously inactive, but began exercising moderately by the time they were over 45 years old. The study found that moderate exercise reduced their risk of death from all diseases by 23 percent.

2. Stop smoking and drinking. While smoking can cause deep wrinkles, drinking can lead to brain damage. Dr. Don Nelson from the University of Cincinnati claims that at age 50 an alcoholic may have the brain of an 80-year-old.

3. Get regular physical checkups. Dr. Ken Cooper, America's leading aerobics expert, is convinced that the leading causes of death in the prime of life are more acts of man than acts of God. Dr. Cooper told *Selling Power* that when a person dies, he dies not so much of the particular disease as of his entire life.

achievement
LESSONS

4. Take your vitamins. Dr. James Enstrom, a medical researcher at UCLA, found that people who took over 300 mg of vitamin C each day lived longer than those who took less than 30 mg.

5. Maintain a positive attitude. Dr. Christopher Peterson, at the University of Michigan, found that a confirmed pessimist is twice as likely to experience minor illnesses as someone with a positive attitude. Dr. Peterson found that pessimists tend to abuse their bodies more, smoke more, drink more and get less sleep than optimists.

6. Learn from disappointments. Dr. Abraham Zaleznik, a psychoanalyst, found that people who handle disappointment well tend to be more successful in life than people who are only preoccupied with success. Try to avoid unrealistic expectations and accept that life does not owe us anything. This insight can often prevent great psychological pain.

7. Exercise self-leadership. In his latest book, *Empires of the Mind* (published by William Morrow), Dr. Denis Waitley suggests that we become the CEO of our own lives. He writes, "Fate is partly the hand you're dealt. You can't control that, but you can control how you play your cards."

8. Stay involved. Dr. Erik Erikson found that vital involvement in old age is a key factor to our longevity. Many people refuse to retire simply because work enhances their will to live. George Burns accepted a booking for his 100th birthday at Caesar's Palace in Las Vegas. What are your plans when you turn 100?

pier but also a longer and more fulfilling life. Downs even shared a personal story about when, contrary to medical dogma, his attitude resolved a seemingly insoluble problem.

"Many of the so-called 'inspirational' books may seem fatuous," Downs says, "but the truth is that they work. People who really take it to heart will be pleasantly surprised that changing an attitude for the better bears fruit in strange ways. Here's an example from my life: When I was young I wore glasses – for about 35 years I think. It didn't matter in radio, but when television came along, I didn't like the way I looked in glasses. I tried contact lenses once, but it felt like stones in my eyes. So I couldn't go that route. I began working without them and I eventually took the attitude that I was going to see without the glasses.

> ## fascinating fact
>
> *The National Science Foundation chose Downs to move the South Pole 33 feet to its new satellite-measured location.*

"And between that and some minor eye exercises from a book, it's been more than 20 years since I put away my last pair of glasses. Besides a little residual astigmatism that I couldn't train myself away from, my eyes are now as good as when I was 15 years old. Now maybe part of that was luck and part is genetic, but I believe that I did it just on attitude."

Some of the major problems facing older Americans today stem from a culture that glorifies youth while stigmatizing the aged. Downs believes that this mentality gained credence in the days when physical strength translated into societal value. "In the frontier days," Downs says, "the usefulness of a person was measured by the ability to chop down trees and build log cabins. Out of this came an accent on youth. But the pendulum has swung too far in that direction. Today there is a lot of prejudice against older people. And, like all victims of prejudice, the victims as well as the perpetrators often subscribe to the prejudice. My father did that. One time when he was in his 80s he had mislaid a checkbook. And he said, 'Damn, I'm getting old.' But I told him, 'Dad, don't talk that way, because I remember you when you were 30 and you forgot more then than you do now.' But when you're 30 and you mislay something, you don't attribute it to getting old."

Downs cautions, however, that people must understand the natural process of aging. "One of the things I seek to avoid in writing about aging," Downs says, "is promoting the idea that as long as you have the right diet, do the right exercise and think right, you'll live forever. Aging is something that happens to everyone at all stages in life. And while there's never anything wrong with getting or being older, there is always something wrong with being injured, ill, discriminated against or alone. But these problems beset people of all ages, not just older people."

This association between aging and reduced mental and physical abilities leads people to draw incorrect or prejudiced conclusions about older people, Downs says. "In our society," he explains, "the people we label as 'old' are often misrepresented as necessarily poverty-stricken, lonely, ailing and inactive. While these conditions do strike older people, as well as people in other age groups, by no means do they reflect the norm among elders.

"Yet we are conditioned to believe that, for example, older people are frail, and old means sickly. But there are no diseases that are age-specific. For example, if all old people were deaf and all deaf people were old, then you would have a disease that was a true concomitant of age. But that's not the case. It's not even the case with Alzheimer's because not all old people get Alzheimer's and Alzheimer's sometimes afflicts people in their 40s. So even though statistically speaking you may be more likely to run afoul of it in old age than in youth, it's still not age-related in that way."

To illustrate his point with an example of someone who hadn't fallen prey to the stereotypical images of the elderly, Downs relates a story he heard about a man who went to the doctor complaining of a bad knee.

"The man had a bad pain in his right knee," Downs says. "And the doctor made some therapeutic recommendations, but ended as doctors often do by saying, 'Now don't expect too much, because of your age and all.' And the man interrupted him and said, 'Doctor, my other knee is also 102 and it doesn't hurt me.' And that points out the right attitude, I think."

INVOLVEMENT

Downs believes that this unwillingness to succumb to pessimism or unflattering stereotypes will help you achieve a fulfilling and productive old age. The final key, he says, is involvement. "I read an interview with an old character actor once," Downs explains, "that crystallized for me the idea that life is enhanced through involvement. He had gone through 700 performances or so of the same play and the interviewer asked if it ever got stale for him. The actor said, 'Well, it probably would if I thought about myself. But for every audience out there it's opening night. I identify with the audience. If I just identified with myself it would have gotten stale before the tenth performance.'

"When I read that I thought, 'Life is like that.' If you focus on yourself it gets stale in a great hurry. But if you're other-directed, and you think about other people and other things, you create an infinite number of concerns, and life is always fresh." In essence, then, whether people face loss, illness or changing circumstances, their success in gaining pleasure in life's latter stages depends on their adaptability to changing circumstances.

> **fascinating fact**
>
> *Downs has been licensed to fly single and multiengine propeller planes, seaplanes, gliders and hot-air balloons.*

"Adaptability is an important thing that most people underestimate," Downs says. "A person who says, 'I don't go on boats because I'm the type of person who gets seasick,' well, they might be right that up until that point they've always gotten seasick when they went on boats, but they shouldn't say that they're that type of person, because it is always up to a person what 'type of' person they want to be. Sometimes you even surprise yourself with what type of person you can be or become."

STRESS REDUCTION

To handle the many emotional and psychological effects of television broadcasting, Downs has taken specific steps that he feels minimize his stress and job-related pressures. "After I had overcome mike fright," he says, "and its television cousin camera fright and made what I felt was a successful transition to television, I began to relax. Above all, I tried to stop worrying about other people's jobs. But there was a time when if a light burned out on the set I was sure it was my fault. Of course, if you are willing to trust others to do their jobs, you run the risk of being called lazy. But the calmer approach has always worked for me – in preservation of health, in audience acceptance and in allowing me to do more than one broadcast series simultaneously – all without burning out."

Downs likes to refer to himself as the world champion dilettante. In addition to holding a Guinness record for amassing 10,000 hours on network commercial television, Downs has, among other pursuits, found time to gain his pilot's license, fly hot-air balloons, dive among sharks along the Great Barrier Reef, sail across the Pacific Ocean, trek to the South Pole in shudderingly Antarctic temperatures, scuba dive for sunken treasure, earn a post-master's certificate in gerontology, write eight books, ride a killer whale and race around the Indianapolis Speedway at 175 mph. In his spare time, Downs also enjoys aerobatics in a glider plane. All this from a man who claims to only enjoy a "moderate" amount of danger.

> ## fascinating fact
>
> In 1972 Downs became national spokesperson for Ford Motor Company.

Whether as a professional broadcaster or during his myriad extracurricular pursuits, Downs has spent a lifetime confronting and overcoming fears. Even in 1939 in his first job announcing for a tiny 100-watt radio station in Lima, Ohio, Downs admits to having suffered from what broadcasters call "mike fright." Whenever the microphone was turned on for the young Downs to introduce a program or sign the station on, he became, in his words, "absolutely terrified." Although he didn't entirely conquer his mike fright until years later, Downs believes that he stuck with broadcasting because he genuinely believed in his own ability and that he had chosen the absolutely right career.

Perhaps because he was at one point the youngest staff announcer hired by a radio network, Downs says he has always been confronted with the idea that he is never old enough to handle a responsibility.

"Strangely, that attitude has stuck with me to this day," he says in his autobiography, *On Camera* (G.P. Putnam's, 1986). "I am now one of the oldest people working full time in a major slot on the air. But there are still times when I think to myself, almost by reflex, 'Maybe I'll let one of the older people take care of that.'"

PHYSICAL ACTIVITY

Downs suggests that another possible explanation for his aging well lies in his unquenchable desire to test himself physically, which has given him a unique perspective among journalists about courage, fear and danger.

"There are people," he says, "who go through life never feeling a need to test themselves physically. Then there are others who live for danger. The human spectrum of challenge runs all the way from fear and timidity about even mild risk to a thirst for danger that can be interpreted as self-destructive.

"I have always felt that our general concept of courage is cloudy, perhaps even false. If someone is truly fearless – so dumb as to not be afraid of anything – then bravery has no meaning. Courage requires that you feel fear and overcome it. To develop a workable way to handle fear, you have to occasionally scare yourself. The process can be pleasant. It's the same sort of pleasure people get out of horror movies or roller coasters.

"At the same time, ignorance often breeds carelessness about things that could reduce risk. If you don't know what you're doing, you're likely to be afraid of the wrong things and careless about the real dangers. In the case of active sports such as blue-water sailing, sky diving, scuba diving, gliding, ballooning and general recreational aviation, the fears are often exaggerated. Statistically, more people die in automobile accidents and from accidents in the home than pursuing recreational activities they may consider dangerous."

But perhaps the true determining factor driving Downs' consistent success has been his ability to sep-

action
PLAN

The Meaning of Life

Unlike many people, Hugh Downs doesn't hem and haw when asked the question of what is the most important thing in life. He provides an extremely detailed response few could dispute.

"I've always separated it into four stages," he says. "If you were coming into the world about to be born and were granted four wishes, you should ask for the following: an unscarred childhood, a zestful and challenging adulthood, a serene old age and a euphoric death. That, I believe, is a sort of utopian goal that everyone strives for in one way or another.

"And I think that some have achieved it. But it requires a bit of good luck as well as some alertness. Someone once said that we bargain for happiness and settle for peace. Which may be true to a certain extent, but at the same time in youth you probably should not dwell too much on the benefits of serenity, because the benefits come when you go out there and really achieve something. That's why I'm all for reminiscing. Why shouldn't a 95-year-old man look back? His whole life is behind him, and he should take both pride and pleasure in that."

arate self from career. "In this country, unfortunately, you always have to 'be' what you do for a living," Downs says. "Which means how you make your living becomes your identity. In other countries you might ask a man what he does, and he might say, 'I write poems' or 'I climb mountains.' Then you find out he is a bank teller.

fascinating fact

In 1965 Downs sailed a boat across the Pacific from Panama to Tahiti.

"Somehow I've never been one to subscribe to the American notion that you are what you do for a living – and God help you if you don't like it. I realize it's important to care about your work, but I've found that in my line of work you also have to relax if you want to do it well. And you have to relax if you plan to stay at it awhile.

"It is a business that can grind on a person in a very destructive way. Since there was nothing else I wanted to do, I built armor against the pressures of broadcasting. I began to take it less seriously and tried to have fun with what I was doing, with the result that I began to do a better job. I came to regard the profession as a means to an end and not an end in itself. My young family was really the center of my life, and my self-identity embraced many activities outside broadcasting."

It seems that for genuine balance in life between career and family, risk and reward and even youth and old age, you could find no better example than Hugh Downs, a man with the courage to live a rich and vibrant life. ▣

Age is only a number, but in selling numbers count. Luckily, Hugh Downs' advice on growing old gracefully is good for both the sales and the soul. To measure how well you apply his lessons to your life, take this quiz and follow the advice next to your scoring range to make sure you only get better with time.

⑤=Always, ④=Often, ③=Sometimes, ②=Rarely, ①=Never

1. I reduce stress regularly by exercising, meditating, reading or engaging in some other relaxing activity.

   ⑤   ④   ③   ②   ①

2. Even when I feel nervous about a call, I am able to put my fear aside and pursue the sale.

   ⑤   ④   ③   ②   ①

3. I am optimistic and try to view problems as opportunities.

   ⑤   ④   ③   ②   ①

4. I avoid stereotyping prospects or customers based on appearance, false information or inaccurate assumptions.

   ⑤   ④   ③   ②   ①

5. I adapt each of my calls to my current buyer and focus on their needs instead of mine.

   ⑤   ④   ③   ②   ①

6. I strive for balance in my life by pursuing interests or hobbies outside of work.

   ⑤   ④   ③   ②   ①

Your Total _____

Your Final Score: Add your score for each question to get your final score. If you scored:

From 25 to 30 points: Your outlook on life should take you far. Setting goals in areas other than sales should help you maintain the balance you have achieved. As you get older, broaden your horizons further with courses on a variety of topics.

From 18 to 24 points: To reduce stress and better understand customers, focus on others instead of yourself. Look for the humor in everyday situations and put your customers first to win more sales and bring more meaning to your position.

Below 18 points: Lighten up a little! Hard work is the key to success, but not every problem you face will make or break your career. Forgive yourself for mistakes, learn from them and move on. Try working for personal satisfaction instead of just money, and develop a social life and interests outside the office.

BETTER SALES ANYONE? TENNIS CHAMP

CHRIS EVERT'S LESSONS IN MENTAL

RESILIENCE AND PREPARATION CAN HELP

YOU ACE MORE SALES CALLS.

PHOTO BY SCHNEPF/GAMMA LIAISON

Chris Evert

Although she may lack superlative athletic ability, great speed or a natural talent for the game of tennis, Chris Evert achieved astonishing success. Any player will tell you Evert often won matches with superior preparation, concentration, focus and a sheer determination to win. In a solitary sport where competitors must rely on self-talk to coach, cajole and motivate themselves for as long as three hours, Chris Evert's mental athleticism represents the true grit against which other champions are measured. Here's how you can learn from her success to improve your mental toughness and close more challenging sales situations.

fascinating fact

In her 19-year career, Chris Evert won 1,309 matches and lost 146.

In 1970 a 15-year-old upstart named Chris Evert burst onto the tennis scene, defeating then-Grand Slam champion Margaret Court at a tournament in Charlotte, North Carolina. No fluke victor or flash in the pan, Evert soon rose to dominate the sport of women's tennis, eventually winning two Australian, seven French, three Wimbledon and six U.S. Open singles titles. In major tournaments Evert's record is an overwhelming 299-37. During her entire 19-year career Chris Evert remained one of the four top-ranked players in the game, a record for longevity that will likely never be challenged by another woman – or man – in tennis or any other sport.

Growing up in South Florida, the eldest daughter of a former tennis champion, Chris Evert spent virtually her entire childhood on the tennis court, drilling, hitting ground strokes and developing every aspect of her tennis game. While her father could teach his daughter all the physical components of the game, only she could control her own attitude. As she wrote in her autobiography, *Chrissy* (Simon & Schuster, 1982): "My dad believed I was born with certain skills. He said, 'Your mom and I can help bring out some of your inherent qualities, but you can't teach somebody to block everything out of his or her mind.'"

This is exactly the skill that analysts highlight when describing Evert's strengths. Concentration has been defined as the ability to focus directly on the immediate moment, not one second in the past or the future, but solely in the right now. This is where Evert excels over opponents.

"Talented players are a dime a dozen," she says. "You can't win on talent alone. Lots of players have more talent than I have. But the thing that separates the good ones from the great ones is mental attitude. It might only make a difference of two or three points in an entire match, but how you play those key points often makes the difference between winning and losing. I'm especially proud that I've been able to win a lot of matches in my career when I've been behind in the third set. I've pulled those matches out because I've hung in. If

To become champion of a Grand Slam tennis tournament, players must defeat seven consecutive opponents, each with a different playing style and range of abilities. During a two-week tournament players can run the full gamut of emotions with any number of peaks and valleys. From match to match winners and losers are often determined not by superior skill or athleticism, but rather by which player has the dedication and resolve to prevail. In many ways, a tennis tournament can be compared to the complex multiple-buyer sale. On the complex sale, salespeople must remain motivated through a drawn out back-and-forth process, while selling to a variety of customers at all levels up and down the corporate chain of command. With many clients the process can take months or even years. Knowing that in sales no one remembers who comes in second place, salespeople should neither be overly encouraged by minor victories nor discouraged by temporary setbacks. This is just as true in tennis. As Chris Evert puts it: "Too many players celebrate after a big victory and lose sight of what's ahead the next day. As a result, they are drained emotionally before they even walk on the court." After a hard-won match, once the handshakes, press conferences and locker room rituals end, in a tournament the tennis player still has to return to the court fully prepared to go through the entire gut-wrenching process again, only this time against an even stronger opponent. Replaying yesterday's victory in your head today will almost surely guarantee you an early exit. A tennis player cannot look beyond an opponent to the finals without first defeating today's opponent. In sales, the competition is as fierce. Only by focusing attention on winning at each step along the way can a sales professional succeed.

achievement
LESSONS

the mind is strong, you can do almost anything you want – it's almost a form of hypnotism."

This superior concentration helps Evert rise to the occasion for important points. In her emotional 2-6, 6-3, 6-3 1986 French Open Finals win over Martina Navratilova, for example, Evert won 65 percent of her service points when the score was close, as compared to merely 33 percent when the points were less crucial.

Mental attitude is just as important in sales as it is in tennis. Although it may only make a difference for a few moments on a sales call or a presentation, superior concentration and focus on the customer can produce dramatic results. Average salespeople often get too absorbed in their presentations and enjoy the sound of their own voices so much that important customer issues go unaddressed. Conversely, top salespeople develop the ability to concentrate and actively listen to customer questions and objections to create positive results for both the customer and the salesperson.

> **fascinating fact**
>
> *Evert is the 163rd person and the 44th woman to be inducted into the International Tennis Hall of Fame.*

DETERMINE YOUR SUCCESS

That Evert won many more three-set matches than she lost is no surprise. Essential to her success has been the determination to win regardless of the match score, opponent or external distractions. While members of the British media dubbed her the "Ice Maiden" for her apparent lack of emotion on the court, in fact they failed to realize that this cool demeanor helped her focus on the task at hand. As a side benefit, Evert's unfazed appearance in the face of challenging points tended to intimidate opponents.

Before matches, Evert sat alone in the locker room with the express purpose of clearing her mind of any distractions. On the court, after each point she held her racquet down and stared at the strings until she was mentally prepared for the next point and knew what she wanted to do. By the time Evert looked up at her opponent, win or lose the last point was already forgotten. Even if she lost the first set of a match, Evert used her opponent's potential letdown to her advantage.

"Too many players lose a close first set and are resigned to believing a match is over," she explains. "I've always taken the opposite approach: 'I've lost the first set, so I'll just have to win the next two.'" Chris Evert has always forced opponents to beat her because she absolutely refuses to defeat herself. When up against the wall at match point, Evert played even more aggressively, as if challenging her opponent to close out the match – or face the consequences.

Like many tennis players, otherwise competent salespeople too often perceive adversity as an inevitable precursor to failure. If a sales call goes poorly in the beginning or a customer seems overly aggressive these salespeople let their self-defeating thoughts bear rotten fruit. Like Chris Evert, however, mentally tough salespeople understand that after a setback, a sales call can go nowhere but up. These superachievers let adversity drive their successes.

fascinating fact

Through Chris Evert Charities Inc., Evert has raised more than $5.5 million to fight drug abuse and assist neglected, drug-exposed and abused children.

GAME, SET AND MATCH – CLOSING THE DEAL

On the flip side of the coin, Evert is also extraordinarily tough with what Arthur Ashe called the hardest part of tennis – putting an opponent away. Almost all players let up some near the end of an easy win, even such hard-nosed competitors as Jimmy Connors and Martina Navratilova. This unconscious drop in concentration leads to common 6-1 and 6-2 set scores. Not so with the relentless Evert. No tennis player has won as many 6-0 sets as this cool competitor with the killer instinct.

Salespeople who demonstrate the killer instinct use trial closes as often as possible so they won't miss an opportunity when the customer is ready to buy. They also pay close attention to body language. When a customer looks puzzled or uninterested, top salespeople stop talking immediately and inquire as to what might be of concern. When all questions and possible objections have been answered, the mentally tough salesperson always asks for the business.

WHILE TIMES CHANGE, CHAMPIONS REMAIN

In her 18 years of professional tennis, Chris Evert observed many dramatic changes in the game she continually struggled to master. Knowing that complacency would relegate her to an early retirement, Evert continued to improve her game throughout her career.

When she was younger, Evert usually cruised with easy victories in the early rounds of tournaments until the semifinals or finals. As the ability gap closed, Evert says she was often forced to test both her physical and mental limits in second- and third-round matches.

To face the increased competition, Evert began training harder and pushing herself more, but also taking more time off to recover from difficult tournaments. To remain competitive in the 1980s Evert had to step up her practice schedule, pushing her body to the point of collapse in the morning, then resting before another exhausting afternoon workout.

She also worked on her tactical game, specifically targeting those skills that needed to improve if she hoped to keep up with the best players. When she joined the pro tour, Evert was a strict baseliner, content to slug it out until her opponents made mistakes. As she faced more serve-and-volleyers, however, Evert realized that she would have to improve her own volleying. In 1983, for every backhand volley she hit for a winner she would miss one. By 1987, that ratio had improved to two winners for every loser, a 100 percent success rate increase.

Although no salesperson can control what the competition does, it is up to the individual to decide how to

action PLAN

1 Sharpen your focus. Her ability to concentrate on the present and block out mistakes and other distractions made a winning difference in Chris Evert's career. To perform at your peak, you have to keep your mind on what you are doing. What can you do to improve your concentration on every call?

2 Get ready to win. As a youngster, winning was easy for Evert. As she got older, though, she had to train harder for endurance and fitness and to strengthen the weaknesses in her game. Sales, too, may be won or lost long before the call. How can you prepare more thoroughly to close more often?

3 Go for the close. Even after taking the lead in a match, Evert didn't take any chances on losing. She continued to give 100 percent until the end of the match. When a call is going well, try to seal the deal. What can you do to close more aggressively in the future?

face the increased challenge. Because she trained harder and smarter, Chris Evert remained a champion longer than anyone else in history.

As Chris Evert proved for 18 years, it is how we face the challenges of tomorrow that separates the average achievers from the champions. ▣

When a tennis match gets grueling, you need mental fitness to match your physical fitness. Chris Evert's single-minded determination, ability to focus and resistance to adversity are as important in the buyer's office as on the court. Even more than tennis, selling is a mental game. Take the quiz below to find out if you are ready to play.

⑤=Always, ④=Often, ③=Sometimes, ②=Rarely, ①=Never

1. I prepare exhaustively for sales calls by researching the prospect and company, polishing my selling skills and getting motivated.

    ⑤   ④   ③   ②   ①

2. I know what areas of my selling skills need improvement, and I follow a strategy to help me get better.

    ⑤   ④   ③   ②   ①

3. On every call, I trial close several times to get the order, and ask for the business directly if the prospect doesn't buy.

    ⑤   ④   ③   ②   ①

4. When speaking with prospects, I don't allow ringing phones, my own errors or other distractions to throw me off track.

    ⑤   ④   ③   ②   ①

5. When a call isn't going as planned, I try harder to get the order, instead of giving up on it.

    ⑤   ④   ③   ②   ①

6. When I see signs that my buyer is interested, I continue to pursue the sale until I have a signed order in hand.

    ⑤   ④   ③   ②   ①

Your Total _____

Your Final Score Add your score for each question to get your final score. If you scored:

From 25 to 30 points: When it comes to selling, you have a one-track mind. To maintain your mental edge, compete with other salespeople and keep improving and learning for continued growth.

From 18 to 24 points: Instead of leaving so much to chance, take control of your sales. Plan your success, then work your plan. Do your homework before every call, and use what you learn. Show buyers you will work hard before you get their business to convince them you will work hard afterward.

Below 18 points: You may be allowing fear to stand in the way of your success. Take responsibility for your sales, and don't be intimidated by VIP buyers. Think of all the problems that worry you during a call, then make a list of measures you can take to prevent them. Never give up on your sale or yourself.

SUBSCRIBE TO THE SALES BASICS THAT

HELPED THE LATE CHAIRMAN MALCOLM KEEP

FORBES IN FRONT, AND WRITE YOUR

OWN SUCCESS COVER STORY.

PHOTO BY ALEXIS DUCLOS/GAMMA LIAISON

Malcolm Forbes

N o one enjoys the fruits of success more than Malcolm Forbes. As testament to that, consider his toys, among them a private stable of 60 to 80 motorcycles and a 151-foot luxury yacht, the *Highlander* – the fifth successive *Highlander* in Forbes' long romance with dining and dealing at sea sports twin Harleys, a Bell Jet Ranger helicopter, Cigarette and Donzi tenders, electronically controlled window shades, gold-plated fixtures, a wine cellar to house part of the Forbes collection of vintage pressed grape, and a small segment of the Forbes art collection including a Raoul Dufy, Thomas Gainsborough, and Henri de Toulouse-Lautrec. It would be easy to stop right here. However, Malcolm Forbes' interests extend far beyond the average perhaps-a-billionaire's purview. (No one knows for sure how much Malcolm S. Forbes is worth. As he says, "No one sees the books.")

However, plenty of folks have seen his Boeing 727, named *Capitalist Tool* after the *Forbes* magazine slogan that has helped bring renewed world respect to the free enterprise system. And many have acquired a piece of his quarter of a million acres in Colorado's Sangre de Cristo mountains. His vast holdings include Trinchera, his family ranch in Colorado; a castle in Morocco; the Chateau de Balleroy in France; an island in Fiji; his 40-acre estate in Far Hills, New Jersey; and the Forbes corporate office complex on lower Fifth Avenue in Manhattan. In addition, of course, there are THE BALLOONS!

As a collector, Forbes is equally indomitable. From the fabulous Faberge

fascinating fact

By age 15, young Malcolm Forbes had published newspapers for his home, school and the Boy Scouts.

eggs (Forbes' collection boasts 12, two up on the Kremlin's 10); toy soldiers (18,000 in the U.S. with the spillover of 128,000 on display in his Moroccan castle); antiques; paintings which include, among others, Renoirs and Van Goghs; an Americana collection which includes autographs from every signer of The Declaration of Independence and the expense account from Paul Revere's midnight ride; and the world's first balloon museum at Forbes' French chateau.

Surveying the entire spectrum of Malcolm Forbes' possessions, acquisitions, pleasures and pursuits, one must also look at his long love affair (just like every other red-blooded boy) with cars. He normally drives an Aston Martin Lagonda, while garaging his Lamborghini Countach with classics like the Cadillac V-16, Twin Six Packard, and a number of Maserati Quattroportes which he has owned over the years.

If the list of Malcolm S. Forbes' possessions is exhaustive, the collector himself is a head-spinning whirlwind of ideas and enthusiasms. His own editorials in the magazine his father founded over 70 years ago hopscotch the political and business checkerboard with stops at any current world or local topic that suits the Forbes fancy. He has built the family publishing business, which he now owns lock, stock and all the toys in the basement, into a major force that rivals and often beats his two giant business magazine competitors.

During the past 20 years, Forbes has met with more than success. As he

achievement LESSONS

"To run a business, someone has to have a sense of marketing. A concept has to spring from a mind; it won't necessarily spring from 100 minds. By marketing I mean selling something. And when you stop and think about it, we're all selling to one degree or another. Anywhere you pull up on a motorcycle, people feel free to talk to you. A car is private. All collections are triggered by nostalgia. Balloons are fun. They make people smile. They're like Christmas tree ornaments floating off the tree.

All I can ask for is to live longer and to enjoy all the good fortune I have now. I'm not in a hurry for the next round — I can't possibly have it as good in the next as I've had it in this! Sharing all this is a big kick. You multiply your own enjoyment when it's shared. My epitaph is already written, 'While alive he lived!'"

once put it, "You can't be successful if you don't love what you're doing. Whatever really turns you on, do it. Psychic income is what real income is used for anyway." And what does mega-wealthy, turned-on Malcolm Forbes love to do? Sell!

The Forbes sales and marketing mechanism, although not obvious to the casual observer, is as well-oiled a piece of machinery as any of the sleek Italian roadsters garaged on his posh estate.

"Anybody in business, if he is going to succeed, is a salesman. Even when he doesn't have a title that relates to sales, or is not conscious of it – everything is selling. Somebody seeking a future in acting has got to sell himself to the producer or the director. There's nothing in life that doesn't involve selling. Including myself as a salesman, it's what makes any business.

"Now, to direct a business like ours – we are selling editorial content to the readers. To do that we have to sell the most capable writers on working for *Forbes*. We have first to be able to sell the people we need to make that business run successfully. Then the advertising, which is the lifeblood of our business, can only be sold when we have the product, which is the editorial. We can sell advertising by being able to point out and stress the value of our product to key decision makers in the marketplace. Everything relates to the bedrock. In our case, first, staff building and second, selling the product based on the fact that it is better and stands up under scrutiny."

> ## fascinating fact
>
> *Forbes won both a Bronze Star and a Purple Heart during World War II.*

Although *Forbes'* competition is stiff, the readership numbers an astounding three quarters of a million subscribers, among whom 250,000 are millionaires. It's a most attractive package to pitch to Madison Avenue.

"In selling, it helps enormously to get in to the decision maker on the buying end. To get in, it helps if they're curious about you. Establishing a name, a persona, is important. People were astonished when Cap Weinberger, the former Secretary of Defense, became our publisher. See, people think a publisher is somebody who comes up through the advertising ranks. But here's a man with complete entree. The end buyer of our advertisers' wares are the people who know Cap Weinberger."

THAT'S ENTERTAINMENT

Malcolm Forbes keeps his name in front of the public with his Friendship Balloon Tours and Goodwill Motorcycle Gang, his flamboyant lifestyle and constant entertaining aboard the *Highlander*.

"In my father's day business journalism was pretty embryonic. And, in those days the press was not as pervasive and powerful as it is today. Business tycoons would only talk to someone they had associated with on their own turf. He would have to be known to them, become a familiar face."

From his father, B.C Forbes, Malcolm learned how to hobnob and he does the same thing now albeit on a grander scale. His well-known lunches at the Forbes townhouse have served for years as the perfect setting to land a lucrative account. The townhouse, where business leaders' own initialed tankards, displayed along the paneled walls, await parched power lips, may have been the setting for the very first power lunch.

Aboard *Highlander*, the same theory applies. Twenty-two-year-old Paul Acken, Forbes Inc.'s seafaring chef, coordinates meals for 120 guests four times per week with gala trips up the Hudson as special events to mark a particularly important sales coup-in-the-making.

"The impression I hope to convey is that the man who has a lot to do with running *Forbes* is alive and aware and informed and I would hope that my customers – that is business leaders – would be willing or curious to break bread with or talk to him. Entree in this case means being able to have these people level with your writers and editors.

"They can't stonewall us. We're writing about them all the time. They can be polite but unforthcoming so we have to see them in a setting that is non-adversarial – not across the desk. We have got to establish rapport. And it goes both ways. The scenario of power is constantly changing. And, in our appraisal of how they are doing with that power, it does a lot to determine whether they

fascinating fact

On November 6, 1973, Malcolm Forbes set the U.S. cross-country balloon flying record, traveling from coast to coast in 21 days.

continue to be people with power.

"So it's not a one-way street where the customer is doing you a favor. It's much more difficult to make the sale if you're constantly depending on favors. It's not enough to have the best product at the best price. You have to be able to get that word out and lay it out. You have to have entree."

Besides entree, *Forbes* offers its audience substance and leadership. For advertisers there are the substantial numbers. And what does it offer Malcolm S. Forbes?

Usually in his office at six a.m. – and by his own admission, it's his favorite place to be. "It's fun to be at your desk when you're the boss," he states.

In his early years, Forbes had ambitions to serve the public. In politics he was a bridesmaid who never caught the bridal bouquet. His terms in the New Jersey State Senate resulted in an unsuccessful bid for governor of that state. Now he has concluded it's more satisfying to be at the controls of his magazine where he can tell other people what they ought to be doing.

Forbes expresses understandable pride in his magazine's slogan, "Capitalist Tool," which pokes good-natured fun at the leftists and, at the same time has helped to reverse a slur on the name of free enterprise.

"That's all capitalism is – free enterprise – although at one time it was an epithet flung at those dubbed robber barons like Carnegie and Rockefeller. Now communist governments are eagerly adopting some form of free enterprise to bolster their collapsing economies. Britain and France are divesting business into private hands because they run it better."

ON THE SELLING ANGLE

Since selling is an ongoing mix of art, science and high style at Forbes Inc., Chairman Malcolm has much to say on the subject. "In selling, your product has got to have differences that are perceived and real. You've got to fill a niche. You've got to point out the difference as a plus. It's infinitely more difficult to compete with something that isn't better or isn't far less expensive. So you've got to have an angle, a twist, a point that differentiates you and then you've got to make the most of it."

action PLAN

The Forbes Formula For Sales Success

▸ Find a way to gain entree.
▸ Differentiate what you sell and point out those differences as a plus.
▸ Don't let success derail your forward momentum.
▸ Analyze your setbacks.
▸ Use disappointments as fuel for growth.
▸ When you have to mention the competition, establish how your product is better.
▸ Selling is not a one-way street where the customer is doing you a favor.
▸ Never forget to ask for the order.

On the competition: "There are circumstances where you don't mention your competition, particularly in consumer products. But when it's a limited field and you go in to sell, say, a copier and you have to differentiate why yours is better than the one they have, you have to mention the competition. You've got to establish how you're better. And then you've got to close the sale by asking for the order. That's an old chestnut that should never be forgotten. A lot of salespeople feel the customer will get the message by osmosis."

On the soft sell: "On the *Highlander* we entertain anywhere from 30 to 50 CEOs and their wives. We talk with different ones about business and the future and we discuss their advertising program. Once when I had heard that the competition was getting more of the client's advertising, I mentioned how foolish I thought it was not to share a message that good with our audience. This particular CEO agreed and said he'd take care of it and he did.

"Over the course of the day aboard the *Highlander* we ask for the order or ask why we didn't get a customer's business. It may take 1 percent of the 14 hours we are together, but we don't forget it.

"It's not a sales call in the classic sense but we do orchestrate an entire event and the people who come to these events know why they are here. The event is the medium's message bearer. Nobody makes a direct pitch, but the whole thing is a pitch. It's a group sell but the real selling is done one-on-one when the salesman with the account calls on the agency media buyers, the account executives and the higher men in the hierarchy call on the directors."

On the team effort: "At our end of the hierarchy we have relationships with the chief executives that we can call when it involves business. We give major sales luncheons, dinners and receptions. Sometimes we give them in a ballroom with a film, remarks by me and forecasts of the economy by my son. Everybody invited is either in the advertising agency, the executive ranks of the company, the VP in charge of sales, the CEO, agency media people and account executives. It's a spectrum where the whole pitch is for business.

"We have about 80 people involved in selling advertising – that includes promotion department, all the people supplying the tools, publishers office and the like. It's a team effort from top to bottom."

THE TYCOON'S TRIALS

The *Forbes* marketing machine, well oiled and heeled, involves far more than the deceptively simple landscape Malcolm S. Forbes paints. Taking into consideration the world-renowned host's many international ballooning and motorcycling pursuits and including extended trips like the 1987 Amazon River expedition aboard the *Highlander*, one is tempted to suggest that Malcolm Forbes has built, not an economic empire, but a state within a corporation, where he is President, Chief of Protocol, and Roving Ambassador, all rolled into the guise of jovial host.

When asked if sometimes he is angered when things don't go his way, Forbes answers with a characteristic Scottish practicality that tells much about why he has come so far with such success.

"I get mad in the sense that, if we didn't do it this year it gets red tagged with how we missed out and why we missed out. And when we go after them next year they become a real target zone. That doesn't mean we always succeed. Some of them take a few years. But the rebuff is never lost. It just means they get twice as much attention. Those setbacks have to give you more energy.

"Of course we often lose business temporarily when we have been critical editorially of a company's policy. People are human and they react by saying, 'Cancel my advertising!' Major companies aren't usually that stupid, but it happens. We don't try to do anything about that except, in due course, we point out that, since they're trying to reach the people who are affected by what we write, it's damn foolish not to be presenting what they have to say to the same people.

"When we suffer a setback, we analyze why we've been outsold or lost the business and then we try to identify the source – the person who said 'no.' Then we go after that person to come for lunch in the townhouse, to sit down with our people. Or we invite them to a function on the *Highlander* where, on certain nights of the week, our advertising department entertains people while the boat cruises around Manhattan.

"We go after these people to get close enough to find out the real reasons we didn't get – or lost – the business and to find out if it's a reason we can correct. Nobody who doesn't analyze the rebuffs can be a successful salesperson.

"The easiest thing to derail salespeople is success. Then they forget to sharpen the pencil. So rebuffs, in many ways, are almost as valuable as the order, if you are to keep honed up, tuned in, turned on."

WHERE THERE'S A WILL

Forbes' self-deprecating and oft-quoted remark that his success is the result of his "ability, spelled i-n-h-e-r-i-t-a-n-c-e," belies a stable disposition, rock solid values, competitive drive and willingness to take carefully measured risks. In addition, every lunch, dinner, event or trip is carefully photographed and catalogued for later proof of its business value. In case the IRS questions who ate the hot peppers that were flown from Bombay aboard the *Capitalist Tool*, Forbes can answer, "One of my customers."

> **fascinating fact**
>
> For his 70th birthday party, Forbes flew approximately 800 people to Morocco for an elaborate party said to cost $2 million.

"The crudest measurement of success is money. We all know that success is a much broader thing than that. For someone born with money, that incentive, the necessity of succeeding, the propulsion, the ambition, in many cases is blunted. When you've got what you need, you don't have the same fires under you and in you. On the other hand, the woods are full of examples of rich men's sons who have been successful. There are plenty of reasons why success in terms of monetary measurement isn't what appeals to lots of people.

"Of course, we're all subject to the temptations of laziness and indulgence.

70

There are few people long happy doing nothing. Doing nothing is the hardest work of all. In my case, at 69, I'm probably busier than ever. I'm very glad that as you get older you need less sleep. You have more things to do because you sense that you're going to run out of time. Retirement kills more people than hard work ever did.

"Disappointments should be utilized. If you're a rejected suitor, well, there's not much you can do about that. But if you're an actor who didn't get the part, then you may learn what you have to do – what is required to get the break you need. Disappointments have a usefulness – if you've never been unhappy how would you know what happy is?

"I was keenly disappointed when I ran for governor of New Jersey three or four decades ago and I was defeated. My father died in the meantime and I found I had to concentrate on the business. I lost my political ambitions and found it was much more fun to be telling people in public office what they should be doing, and being sought by them for support, than by spending all my time listening to advice and seeking support."

Forbes seems to have little, if any, remorse. Of the disappointments he has suffered, most recently the breakup of his 39-year marriage, he takes a characteristically pragmatic approach and says without rancor or regret, "After 39 years of entertaining, my wife finally said she'd had enough. She wanted to live out the rest of her days the way she chose. She never liked being in the public eye and she now spends much of her time on her ranch."

As usual, Forbes transcended that disappointment and made lemonade by squiring a lady whose persona is even more celebrated than his own.

With Malcolm S. Forbes everything seems to work out so right. Never mind the endless work, the constant stroking of clients, the management of his empire, the high-tension activities that would wear out a lesser being, and the incredible diversification of his already vast portfolio. Never mind that, while globe-trotting, cruising the Amazon, ballooning across America and everywhere else in the world or road rallying with The Goodwill Motorcycle Gang, he still finds time to run an incredibly successful publishing business. Never mind that the business, under his ownership, has grown far beyond what his father could have imagined into one of the most influential and interesting publications on the market today.

Yet there he is. It's six a.m. and Malcolm's taking notes for his next editorial, analyzing why a big fish slipped out of his net and watching what the competition is doing. He realizes that if you're in the game, you've got to play to win. The only way to do that is the professional way. Cover all your bases and watch the pitching signals. Remember the basics and have some fun while you work.

Forbes' fun is his work. Everytime he goes out to have fun, that, too, becomes another function of Forbes Inc. The real kicker is...he's making as much money from the pleasures of his pursuits as he ever made pursuing them in the first place. ▣

Forbes' sales calls may resemble *Lifestyles of the Rich and Famous*, but you don't need big bucks to win big sales. Instead, follow Malcolm's formula: Treat customers well, learn from setbacks and ask for the sale. Take the quiz below to see how well your sales strategy matches Forbes', then use the tips in your scoring range to amass your own small fortune.

⑤=Always, ④=Often, ③=Sometimes, ②=Rarely, ①=Never

1. I do my best to provide products, service and personal attention that make my buyers feel special.

    ⑤   ④   ③   ②   ①

2. I use a specific strategy to gain entrée and build rapport with buyers.

    ⑤   ④   ③   ②   ①

3. I can compare my products to my competitors' and show buyers why mine are superior.

    ⑤   ④   ③   ②   ①

4. I am not afraid to ask for the order directly.

    ⑤   ④   ③   ②   ①

5. When I suffer a setback, I am determined to rise above it and maintain my progress.

    ⑤   ④   ③   ②   ①

6. I work as a team with people outside my department to offer customers a seamless sales and service experience.

    ⑤   ④   ③   ②   ①

Your Total _____

Your Final Score Add your score for each question to get your final score. If you scored:

From 25 to 30 points: You're well on your way to Forbes-scale success. In sales, substance should take precedence over style, so remember what will matter to your customers in the long run and continue to provide it.

From 18 to 24 points: Remember that understanding the basics only helps your sales if you implement the techniques consistently. All your prospects are worthy of your best effort, so give it to them. For each simple technique, make a short list of ways to implement it in actual selling situations and practice to refine your performance.

Below 18 points: You need a refresher course on elementary selling skills to strengthen your foundation. Get a good book that covers all the elements of the sales process and study it. Ask for some one-on-one time with your manager and work together to design a beginning-to-end selling strategy that will help you reach your potential.

STEP INTO THE RING WITH BOXER-CUM-

SALESMAN GEORGE FOREMAN AND LEARN

TO ROLL WITH THE PUNCHES AND TKO

YOUR COMPETITORS.

PHOTO BY WESTENBERGER/GAMMA LIAISON

George Foreman

I n 1987, following an unprecedented 10-year absence from the ring, former heavyweight champion George Foreman returned to professional boxing with one goal: to recapture the title he had lost 14 years earlier to Muhammad Ali. Despite Foreman's newfound easygoing manner and upbeat attitude, George-bashing quickly became the number one pastime among sportswriters.

Chiding him as too old, too fat and too slow to keep up with the new generation of boxers, most pundits took umbrage at the bald, grinning, chunky Foreman's reemergence on the boxing scene. And what of his pledge to once again wear the champion's belt? With not-so-thinly veiled references to Foreman's increasing girth most analysts' only response was "fat chance."

But a funny thing happened on the way to Foreman's assured humiliation. He started winning. Then he kept on winning. By 1991 Foreman had won 24 straight bouts, 23 of them by knockout. Even after losing a tough 12-round decision in a 1991 championship bout with Evander Holyfield, Foreman persevered to gain another shot at the title. In 1994, at the long-over-the-hill age of 45, George Foreman knocked out then-titleholder Michael Moorer to become, once again, heavyweight champion of the world.

Today, some of the same experts who once decried Foreman's return laud him as a hero for the fortysomething set – a man who defied the odds, the aging process and all the fitness experts, eating his way up a mountain of cheeseburgers to find redemption and championship winnings at the top.

> ## fascinating fact
>
> *Clay Hodges is the only boxer to defeat George Foreman twice.*

75

That image certainly meshes with Foreman's public persona, his self-deprecating humor and jokes about his opponents. But behind all the bluster and self-promotion lies the true George Foreman, a man whose relaxed style belies a life spent battling demons, pushing himself to the edge and overcoming obstacles through renewal.

READY TO RUMBLE

Foreman's story began in the ghetto of Houston's notorious Fifth Ward, also known as the Bloody Fifth. There he grew up the fifth of seven children being raised by a single mother, often on as little as $26 a week. As a teenager, Foreman fit the profile of a typical inner-city tough, with few marketable skills and even fewer prospects.

fascinating fact

Foreman went on a 21-day "prophet's fast" as a result of a vision.

Dropping out of school in the 10th grade, young George was soon drinking excessively, mugging pedestrians and brawling with anyone who looked at him sideways. According to brother Roy, George's size was so intimidating that he never even bothered to carry a weapon. Foreman's heroes reflected this violent, dead-end lifestyle.

"I thought a hero was a guy who came back from prison," Foreman told *Esquire* magazine, "with a scar down his face, maybe killed a guy once. Can you imagine my goal was to have a scar down my cheek?" Foreman even took to wearing a Band-Aid on his cheek until the day when he could uncover a real scar of his own.

Perhaps his life of crime could have gone on forever except for one fateful day after a mugging, Foreman sought refuge from the police and their pursuit dogs in the mud beneath a house. He remained in the cold and dark down in the mud for hours listening to the dogs barking and imagining himself cowering thus for the rest of his life. At that moment something snapped in Foreman. He saw a life going nowhere, a life of hiding and fear. This experience, he says, forced him to realize that he had become a common criminal. If he didn't change his life for the better, he realized, he would soon be in prison or dead.

achievement LESSONS

George Foreman gives credit for a great deal of his recent successes to a vastly improved attitude. When he first retired from boxing in 1977 Foreman was surly and extremely sensitive to criticism. Today he exudes positive energy and ignores the nattering nabobs of negativity. As he explained to *Men's Health* magazine this new attitude now permeates every aspect of his training — and his life.

"You can say to me, 'George, I'm gonna make your jab faster,'" he explained. "But I will totally object to you telling me my jab is slow. You have to shut out negativity."

Foreman's beliefs about aging and exercise reflect this belief that every individual controls his or her physical destiny.

"If you exercise consistently," he says, "that's the pot of gold that will give you another 20 years. The human body is the greatest machine of all, because it can keep getting better. The dent I made in sports is going to be a drop in the bucket compared to what will happen in the next 20 years. Athletes are going to be performing better than they were at 21 or 22, and it's not going to be a knock on the youngster. It's going to be a blessing."

More than anything else, however, Foreman believes that a positive attitude helps people handle life's inevitable setbacks.

"Nothing happens for the worst if you keep living," he says. "There's a time you can say that, then there's a time you can assume that, but then as you grow older, especially in sports and in life, you know that. It becomes your knowledge."

Foreman's saving grace came in the Job Corps, a program created under President Lyndon Johnson to help young people develop job skills.

There he met Doc Broadus, who took George's natural talent for pummeling people and honed it into a true boxing proficiency. By 1968 Foreman had risen through the amateur ranks to win the right to represent the United States at heavyweight in the Mexico City Olympics. He then shocked the entire boxing world by besting all en route to winning the gold medal.

Foreman's stunning victory was overshadowed by politics. While sprinters Tommie Smith and John Carlos held their fists aloft in the black power symbol as "The Star-Spangled Banner" played, Foreman instead celebrated his victory by waving a small American flag at the crowd. He says the gesture was taken to mean something he had never intended.

"When I was jumping up and down, waving that little American flag," he said, "they thought I was rejecting the climate there. I wasn't. For the first time, I had an identity. I belonged to a country."

CHANGE OF HEART

Upon turning professional, Foreman used his rage, propensity for brawling and devastating knockout punch to plow through opponents. By 1973 he gained a title shot, against Smokin' Joe Frazier in Jamaica. In just two rounds Frazier was out cold, lifted off his feet and onto the mat by a punishing Foreman uppercut. Despite the fight's quick result, and contrary to appearances, Foreman says that entering the ring he was terrified of Frazier.

"I'd seen him fight Buster Mathis like a Pac Man," Foreman said. "I'd seen him stay on Ali's chest like a conqueror. Boxers see things like that. Man, I just wanted to get out of there alive. Going into the ring, my knees shook like I was in an earthquake. I couldn't stop them. I threw all that sick fear at Frazier."

Foreman's title was short-lived, however. The following year, Ali bounced around the ring with his so-called rope-a-dope strategy, avoided Foreman's powerful punches and eventually put Foreman to the canvas in the eighth round. The loss sent Foreman into a downward spiral of anger, brooding and paranoia that bottomed out after a tough loss to Jimmy Young in Puerto Rico.

fascinating fact

As a child, poverty forced Foreman to wear donated second-hand clothes. He mended holes in his shoes with cardboard.

In the locker room after the fight, Foreman faced at once the most terrifying and emancipating experience of his life. He claims he saw blood oozing out of his forehead, hands and feet and that, as he puts it, "Jesus came alive in me. I literally died. All I saw was hopelessness under my feet, over my head total darkness. There was the smell of death. It still makes me nervous to think about it."

That fight and his subsequent conversion experience occurred in 1977. Immediately following that night Foreman decided to dedicate his life to God. He returned to Houston, first as a lay street preacher, then later as an ordained nondenominational minister.

Recalling his troubled youth, Foreman used his substantial influence, name recognition and financial wherewithal to develop the George Foreman Youth and Community Center as a magnet for Houston's troubled kids. Ironically, it was just this newfound dedication to the community and its kids that drove Foreman back to boxing. Realizing that he could make more money for the center in the ring than by doing hundreds of personal appearances, Foreman agreed to once again strap on the gloves and stage the unlikeliest comeback in boxing history.

Unlike other returning champions, however, Foreman set his own agenda and pace.

"I knew it would take fights over a long period of time to do it right," Foreman told *The New York Times*. "I'd seen others like Muhammad Ali and Joe Frazier fail in their comebacks because they were looking for overnight success. I treated myself like a young man, a prospect."

He called this process "puddle-hopping" – fighting light competition in such far-flung boxing meccas as Sacramento, Orlando and Anchorage, all the while building to a title shot against then-champ Mike Tyson. While the sportswriters denigrated Foreman's competitors as palookas, he ignored the naysayers and continued ballyhooing his barnstorming tour, fighting about once every six weeks. Most important, palookas or not, Foreman kept delivering knockout punches. It seems he was fighting for a greater cause that gave his punch extra power.

He also developed an ingenious method for handling the critics. Rather than trying to combat their slurs on his weight, age and opponents, Foreman started cracking jokes at his own expense. To criticism of the caliber of his opponents Foreman would reply, "There are some who claim I don't fight a guy unless he's on a respirator. That's a lie. He has to be at least eight days off the respirator."

On his age and weight Foreman was equally candid. "I should be carrying a cane," he quipped. "My training camp is Baskin-Robbins. But if Tyson wins, it's only Lamborghinis and big houses for himself. Means nothing. If I win, every man over 40 can grab his Geritol and have a toast."

Not only did George win over the critics with this new attitude, he also began winning over fans in droves. With each knockout he became a more omnipresent advocate for the middle-aged. With a Bible in one hand and a cheeseburger in the other he would declare, "Forty is no death sentence. Age is only a problem if you make it one."

action PLAN

1 Make the effort. Of all the success predictors—attitude, ability, intelligence — effort may be most important. Foreman followed a tough training regimen to make his comeback — an example you should follow to outsell competitors. What can you do to make more calls and spend more time in the trenches instead of doing paperwork or traveling?

2 Face your fear. Foreman admits he was terrified to fight Joe Frazier for his first title, yet he defeated him in just two rounds. Almost all salespeople face fear, but the great ones don't let it stop them. How can you better understand and overcome your fears to build your selling momentum?

3 Believe in yourself. Plenty of people told him he couldn't, but Foreman knew he could. How can you boost your intake of motivational material and improve your self-talk to reaffirm your faith in yourself?

FIGHTING FOR RESPECT

Rather than taking criticism to heart, George embraced it. If people wanted to poke fun at a man who named his sons George Jr., George III, George IV and George V, that was fine with George Sr. Foreman took advantage of the publicity, appearing with all four sons in a TV commercial for Doritos.

Taken together, the barnstorming, bluster and humor all served one unifying purpose: to bring public attention back to George Foreman. Understanding that the only bad publicity is no publicity, Foreman did whatever he felt was necessary to make a spectacle of himself.

"When I was a little boy," he explains in his autobiography, *By George* (Villard Books, hardcover, $23), "street cleaners came by the house. Nobody paid attention. But let that fire truck come by. They all rushed out, chased it in pajamas, women with hair rollers. Well, I'm a fire truck. I'm happening. You're all going to be chasing me because you know there's a fire ahead of me somewhere."

But Foreman knew the fire truck would have to do more than swap jokes with the media and spout positive aphorisms to regain the title. Contrary to the Burger King/Baskin-Robbins public persona, Foreman dropped from his prereturn weight of 315 pounds to a more svelte 250 on a diet of fruits, vegetables, pasta, chicken and only the occasional treat.

"If I've been training for five straight weeks, and I'm starting to get grouchy, I'll go for the ice cream," he says. "Or if I feel like eating five cheeseburgers, I'll eat five cheeseburgers. I live by my cravings. Whenever I crave something, I know I should have that. But I use it as a training technique – as a reward."

Compared to Evander Holyfield's carefully sculpted physique, aesthetically speaking, Foreman's body-in-the-round style still gives weight trainers shivers. Even today he tips the scales at well over his preretirement 217-pound mark. Not a problem, he tells anyone who will listen.

"What you have to do to get those designer bodies will get you killed," he argues in *By George*. "You've got to have a body built for boxing, built for fighting and surviving, and I've got that body. There's safety in being bigger. I'm a bigger man and other guys have to get out of my way. You ever notice how the guys you see lying flat on their back and knocked out – the guys you have to pump back to life – all have ripples down their stomach? Boxing is physical fitness, not beauty. And I'm the most physically fit guy on the scene."

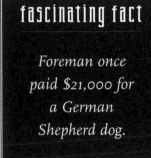

fascinating fact

Foreman once paid $21,000 for a German Shepherd dog.

Foreman may be right. What he lacks in muscle tone he more than compensates for in endurance. His self-constructed workout regimen is the stuff of legends. For two hours, Foreman will run behind a pickup truck loaded with a heavy punching bag. While running he intermittently weaves, jabs, punches and ducks, simulating action in the ring. Ten miles down the road he fits himself into a harness and drags the truck back for half a mile. His gym workouts are similarly intense. For an hour solid he will throw lefts at a punching bag then, at the sound of a timer, switch to throwing rights for another hour. With no rest in between, Foreman frequently spars with a variety of opponents, often for as many as 25 rounds. Add some serious weight training, wood chopping and jumping rope until the wee hours into the mix and in a nutshell you've got the George Foreman workout program.

Only when he talks about his training does Foreman mention the concessions he has made to age. Rather than admit deficiencies, however, the ever-upbeat George says he merely redoubles his efforts.

"I've had to train twice as hard as I did when I was young," he allows. "I don't have all the so-called youth to depend on, so now I depend on skill and conditioning. I knew coming back that if I got knocked down in the ring, the referees in their kindness and compassion would say, 'Stop!' So my legs need to be much stronger than they were when I was young. That's why no one knocks me down."

Even if the redoubtable George had failed in his quest to regain the championship, by any other yardstick he has become an unqualified success. No longer the distant, angry thug the fans loved to hate, Foreman has been reborn in every way. Instead of taking out his pent-up aggression and rage on anyone who dares get in his way, the new George Foreman says he is full of love for everyone. And the public loves him back.

Since his triumphant return to the spotlight, Foreman has starred in the eponymous situation comedy *George*, announced fights at ringside for HBO, written a bestselling autobiography and endorsed more products than anyone this side of Bill Cosby. Along the way Foreman has developed his own theory about what it takes to succeed in sales, and why people find him so convincing.

"I learned something early in life," he told *The Washington Post*. "If you sell, you'll never starve. In any other profession, you can find yourself out on the street, saying, 'They don't want me anymore.' But if you learn the art of selling, you will never go hungry."

"In time," he says in his autobiography, "I think I became the best salesman around, not because I'm a better actor, but because I'm not. What I do is fall in love with every product I sell. If I can't fall in love with it I don't sell it." Foreman also says that people know when you make claims you don't personally believe. Honesty, says Foreman, sells. "Nobody seems to doubt that the George Foreman they see on the screen is the real George Foreman. Everyone thinks they know me. They do," says the man who has broken myth after myth in a legendary boxing career.

Looking ahead, no one, perhaps including George himself, knows exactly what the future will hold for George Foreman. Since winning the title he has fought one defense, winning a 12-round decision over Germany's Axel Schultz. But rather than fight Schultz again, Foreman has agreed to give up the title, possibly to set up a rematch with Michael Moorer. And of course, hanging over every boxing decision Foreman makes is the omnipresent question of retirement. When asked about hanging up the gloves again he usually replies with the quintessential George Foreman humor: "The usual retirement age is 65," he says, "but I'm not going beyond 63. I thought about 65, but that's just too long. I'd say 63." ◨

Even if you never strap on a pair of gloves at the Garden, you go 13 rounds with your competitors every day. With the skill and mental toughness that made George Foreman a world champion, you can deliver your own knockout selling punch. Use the test below to reveal just how much more training you need to claim your own sales title.

⑤=**Always,** ④=**Often,** ③=**Sometimes,** ②=**Rarely,** ①=**Never**

1. Even when the odds seem against me, I believe in myself and practice constructive self-talk.

       ⑤   ④   ③   ②   ①

2. I can feel anxiety about a call or an appointment without letting it sabotage my performance.

       ⑤   ④   ③   ②   ①

3. I understand that success takes time, and I have goals with reasonable deadlines to keep me on schedule.

       ⑤   ④   ③   ②   ①

4. I avoid negative people and refuse to be brought down by others' bad attitudes.

       ⑤   ④   ③   ②   ①

5. I consistently put in the hours and the effort that my goals require.

       ⑤   ④   ③   ②   ①

6. I don't rest on my laurels; when I reach one goal, I set another more challenging one.

       ⑤   ④   ③   ②   ①

Your Total _____

Your Final Score Add your score for each question to get your final score. If you scored:

From 25 to 30 points: You have the skills of a champion and the attitude to match. When more difficult times put your toughness to the test, remember what's gotten you this far and you'll pass with flying colors.

From 18 to 24 points: To reach your potential, make more than a half-hearted attempt. Motivation fuels your efforts, so boost your desire to win and your faith in yourself with daily 30-minute motivation sessions, then follow up with action. Design a sales plan with goals and action steps and show it to your manager so you can both track your progress.

Below 18 points: You may want to be a top achiever, but don't know if you have what it takes or where to begin. First, assess your attitude and ability. If you lack skill and confidence, remember that other top salespeople have felt the same way. Next, have your manager provide training to improve your attitude and your skills. Supplement your training with books on specific topics or techniques that interest you most.

OPPORTUNIST BILL GATES PLAYS HARDBALL

TO SELL SOFTWARE. UPGRADE YOUR SUCCESS

BY MAKING HIS VISION, TIMING AND ENERGY

PART OF YOUR SALES STRATEGY.

PHOTO BY B. LITTLE/SYGMA

Bill Gates

D epending on whether they're Bill Gates supporters or one of his many detractors, Gates watchers refer to Microsoft's chairman as either a nerdy overachiever; grown-up boy genius; shrewd businessman; lucky opportunist; cutthroat competitor; brilliant visionary; or high-tech robber baron. Take your pick. Lodged somewhere among these myriad characterizations lies the truth about America's youngest billionaire, the wunderkind of the software industry.

Say what they will, no one questions that today 38-year-old Gates, with over $39 billion in assets and the richest man in America, sits atop the multibillion-dollar computer industry mountain that only two decades ago existed solely in the minds of a few forward-thinking electronics buffs. With tremendous determination, a legendary work ethic, shrewd business savvy and pure sales genius, in 20 years Bill Gates has grown the company from a one-customer, two-man operation run between college semesters into the world's largest software producer. Fiscal 1998 revenues topped the $14 billion mark with a net income of $4.49 billion.

As an eighth-grade student at Seattle's tony private Lakeside School, Bill Gates helped fill out the slide-rule-wearing math-science crowd. Neither popular nor athletic Gates was already impressing students and teachers with his formidable brain power. That year Gates and his math-science classmates encountered Lakeside's new ASR-33 Teletype computing machine. Almost instantly the soon-to-be-13-year-old Gates was hooked.

As their expertise grew, the programming-literate Lakeside students wanted

> ## fascinating fact
>
> *Microsoft's net revenue for the fiscal year ending June 1997 totaled $11,360,000,000.*

more computer time than Lakeside could accommodate. As a solution they arranged to work debugging the University of Washington Computer Center's more powerful computers in exchange for free programming time. With such time costing up to $4.80 a minute, the young whizzes felt they had hit the mother lode.

In 1970, under the highfalutin' rubric of Lakeside Programmers Group, four Lakeside students – Paul Allen, Ric Weiland, Kent Evans and 15-year-old Gates – sold their programming services to Information Systems Inc. to write a payroll program for the Portland, Oregon, company, once again in exchange for free computer time. When ISI later tried to back out of the deal, Gates and Evans went to Bill Gates Sr., attorney-at-law, to help straighten things out.

fascinating fact

Bill Gates read the entire World Book encyclopedia – A through Z – by age nine.

By the spring of 1973 Gates had cut his teeth programming for both ISI and TRW and even, with Paul Allen, begun a fledgling traffic-counting business called Traf-O-Data. As he focused his attention on college, young Bill set about selling himself to admissions officers at Harvard, Yale and Princeton. His application process tells volumes about Bill Gates' intuitive sales ability. To Harvard, he portrayed himself as the son of a lawyer with an interest in law and politics, playing up his internship as a page the previous summer in Washington, D.C. To Princeton, Gates was the self-proclaimed computer nerd who scored a perfect 800 on the math SAT and could program like a magician. For Yale, he remade himself once again as a former Boy Scout with a healthy interest in acting and the arts. For the man who would later sell himself to the likes of Apple, IBM and NEC, the Ivy League was a snap. Gates was accepted to all three and decided on Harvard.

At Harvard, Gates worked on his soon-to-be-renowned debating skills, arguing with fellow students about everything from books and movies to the future of technology. Although some disagreed, Gates believed that someday every home would have a computer that would handle virtually any task from household finances to teaching children to read.

THE LANGUAGE OF SUCCESS

Gates' vision received a major boost in December 1975 when former Lakeside pal and then-Harvard student Paul Allen excitedly approached Bill to show him the January issue of *Popular Electronics* magazine. The cover story featured the Altair 8800 from MITS Inc., proclaiming it the "World's First Minicomputer Kit."

Allen and Gates agreed that if they wanted to ride the crest of the computer revolution, they would have to be first to write a BASIC computer language to run on the Altair, which would make the machine into something more than a box with blinking lights. On Traf-O-Data letterhead, the two wrote a sales letter to the Albuquerque-based MITS claiming to have already written a BASIC for the Altair. Despite some confusion when MITS president Ed Roberts telephoned the Seattle number on the letterhead and spoke to the befuddled mother of one of Bill and Paul's Lakeside buddies, Allen eventually contacted Roberts, who requested that the two come to Albuquerque in a month to try out their BASIC.

Inaugurating a tradition that would repeat itself later at Microsoft, the eager programmers set about writing the code (jargon for programming) they had claimed to have finished already. This sold-but-not-yet-written product type would later acquire the label "vaporware." Virtually ignoring their classes, and without a single Altair as a reference, Gates, Allen and freshman accomplice Marty Davidoff went into hard-core programming mode. As the date of Allen's departure arrived, the code was done, although on the airplane Allen realized that they had forgotten to write the simple but essential loader program. Without it the machine would never run. With true code-writing aplomb, Allen wrote the entire program by the time the plane landed in Albuquerque.

The next day at MITS headquarters the BASIC, despite numerous bugs which had yet to be worked out, ran successfully on the Altair. Ecstatic, in July 1975, the precocious programmers signed a contract to work with the rapidly expanding MITS. For both men the contract meant entree into legitimate paying jobs doing something – writing code – they would probably have done anyway for fun. Although Gates would return to Cambridge for two more half-hearted semesters, the contract with MITS spelled an end to his college career.

By 1977 Gates and Allen had both moved to Albuquerque permanently and begun calling their byte-size partnership Microsoft. They had sold minicomputer languages for microprocessors to such companies as Tandy, ADDS, General Electric and an upstart California company named Apple Computers.

As the minicomputer business showed signs of growth, so did a problematic development that would continue to plague the software industry: software theft. Rather than pay for programs which many felt should be in the public domain, users often simply copied BASIC from one another. This practice cut directly into Microsoft's profits, sacred ground to Gates.

In an industry newsletter Gates wrote "An Open Letter To Hobbyists," decrying the piracy and criticizing any who would engage in it. Although the letter would do little to stem the tide of stolen programs, it increased Gates' name recognition among the national computer literati and initiated the process of name association between Gates and Microsoft.

By the end of 1978, Gates the rapidly maturing software magnate was 23 and Microsoft's business was booming. For the first time the company cleared over $1 million in sales and had set its sights on moving to the old Gates

Gates' Golden Rule: Do unto competitors before they do unto you. In selling as in software, time is of the essence. Over and over, Bill Gates proved success comes not just from doing a job better than competitors, but doing it faster. Take a lesson in timing from Gates and remember: When you act may be as important as how you act.

Answer opportunity's knock NOW. Knowing every moment counted, Gates sold the BASIC language for the MITS Altair in 1975 before it was even written. His speed paid off and he got the contract to work with MITS. Make your own opportunities when you can, but when one falls in your lap, don't hesitate to make the most of it.

achievement
LESSONS

Do the time. Gates is famous for his work ethic, and although long hours may not top your list of favorite things, overtime can help improve your timing by ensuring that you are prepared when opportunities arise.

Keep yourself organized and beat competitors to the punch. Gates' agreement with IBM in 1981 didn't prevent him from selling his languages elsewhere. To help make MS-DOS the standard, he lowered the up-front fee for those who bought immediately – a technique that helped stifle competitors. Know what your competition is up to and get the jump on them to stay a step ahead.

stomping grounds, the Pacific Northwest or, more specifically, Bellevue, Washington, home of the new Microsoft headquarters.

In practice, little about the way Microsoft operated had changed since Gates' Harvard days. Microsoft would sell a customer on a product it had yet to develop, then super-talented programmers would put in mind-numbing hours writing code to get the project finished on time.

Casual attire, unkempt beards, fast food, soda and office catnaps were the rule of the day. If you couldn't handle this environment then you didn't belong at Microsoft. Despite this patently irregular business environment, through talent and commitment Microsoft gained a reputation for delivering on promises where so many other software companies failed.

In 1979 Microsoft's success reached the ample ears of H. Ross Perot, who expressed an interest in buying Microsoft. Although the deal fell through over money, Perot would later express regret about not taking Microsoft at any price.

MAKING IT BIG WITH BIG BLUE

Gates knew that to grow, Microsoft needed a more focused organizational chart and administrative system. All 26 employees at least nominally still reported directly to the chairman and the company's books were kept on hand-written ledgers. For help Gates turned to Harvard buddy and Stanford Business School student Steve Ballmer, who became Microsoft's assistant to the president. Just in time too. On Tuesday, July 22, two IBM executives came to Bellevue to meet with Gates about a top-secret minicomputer project Big Blue had in development. IBM representative Jack Sams was surprised to find out that the office boy, an apparent teenager in a suit a few sizes too large was, in fact, Bill Gates. With his superior knowledge and keen intuitive grasp of the industry, Gates soon made it clear that he was in charge.

By August, Microsoft signed an agreement to supply IBM with its whole line of languages and find an operating system powerful enough to run on the proposed computer, the IBM PC. After some searching which led him down to Silicon Valley and back to Washington State, Gates eventually located Seattle Computer and its QDOS, short for Quick and Dirty Operating System. Microsoft paid Seattle

Computer $75,000 for the rights to QDOS, which in a later incarnation would become MS-DOS, and told IBM they could do business. On November 6, 1980, Ballmer and the 25-year-old Gates arrived at Big Blue's headquarters in Boca Raton, Florida, and, after a brief detour to buy Gates a tie, signed the contract that would help make Microsoft one of the world's wealthiest companies.

This was by far the biggest enterprise Microsoft had taken on in its six-year history. Although the small company was already swamped with business and struggling to stay on top of the massive workload, Gates could not pass on this opportunity to hitch Microsoft's wagon to the potential IBM PC juggernaut. On August 12, 1981, to much fanfare, IBM proudly announced the IBM Personal Computer, which, with the help of a growing Seattle-area software company, would revolutionize the world more than a little.

fascinating fact

From 1988 to 1993, Microsoft's head-count more than quintupled, rising from 2,793 to 14,430.

Even then Gates knew that the key to software success lies in insinuating your product into every corner of the market, in effect, to become the industry standard. This has been the dominant precept driving Gates' vision to make Microsoft the "IBM of software." Ironically, in time Big Blue would play a major role in fulfilling Gates' ambition.

Because selling its languages to IBM did not prohibit Microsoft from selling to anyone else who came calling, Microsoft used the IBM contract to leverage other computer manufacturers into buying MS-DOS and other Microsoft products. In addition, to establish MS-DOS as quickly as possible, Gates offered the operating system for an unusually low up-front fee, but only if you acted immediately. This lowballing technique, which effectively marginalized competitors' products, would become a regular feature of the Bill Gates selling arsenal.

All of these tactics have helped build and sustain the unstoppable Microsoft steam train. One need only look to the now-common phrase "No one ever got fired for buying Microsoft" to understand that Microsoft has realized Gates' vision to become the "IBM of software."

WINDOWS OF OPPORTUNITY

Although Microsoft was then working with Apple to create the incredibly user-friendly Macintosh computer platform, by autumn 1982 the Mac's release was still a year away. Certainly no one was near an easy-to-use universal platform for the PC. Or so Gates thought. The 1982 Comdex show provided Gates with a rude awakening. There attendees caught a glimpse into the future with a Graphical User Interface (GUI, pronounced "gooey") product called VisiOn. Created by the popular VisiCalc spreadsheet's parent company, VisiCorp, VisiOn was an all-in-one integrated software system running – to Gates' horror – on the PC.

For the end user VisiOn provided a simulated desktop platform which would act as a buffer between the operating system and applications. What it meant to Microsoft, if successful, was that someone else would provide the industry standard for which all PC software companies would write applications. If VisiOn succeeded, Gates' dream for a computer in every home might become a nightmare for Microsoft. The unchallenged king of DOS and BASIC didn't even have a competing platform in production. No matter. The Smart Guys at Microsoft always operated best under combat conditions. Because VisiOn was still at that time only a demo, Microsoft had room to maneuver. The plan went as follows: First, create a team to work on a spec for Microsoft's quickly named Interface Manager; second, saturate the market with the news that Microsoft had an even better windowing environment, as they were known, waiting in the wings. Every salesperson should let flow a deluge of Interface Manager to all potential customers to get their commitments. Third, Gates himself would get IBM and other big clients on board.

As with selling BASIC to MITS, Microsoft again went into pitch mode, selling Interface Manager despite having nothing but a hastily thrown together "smoke-and-mirrors" demo that looked good but had no actual functionality. Writing code could wait; pre-empting VisiOn was the crucial task at hand. Marketing whiz Rowland Hanson came on board in mid-1983, changed Interface Manager's name to Microsoft Windows and began targeting magazine editors to improve Microsoft's public relations.

By Comdex 1983 Windows was everywhere. Microsoft assembled 23 DOS licensees at the press briefing including Compaq, Digital and Hewlett-Packard to pledge their support. Magazines trumpeted its imminent arrival while Comdex attendees saw Windows paraphernalia everywhere. All this for a nonexistent product. It was classic Gates chutzpah.

While hyping Windows may have been a simple marketing ploy, the actual programming wasn't quite so easy. By the already often-postponed release date in November 1984, Windows was farther along, but still nowhere near ready to ship. Due to a prohibitive price tag and a slow, bug-filled code VisiOn had faded from the scene, but in the meantime Boston-based Lotus, producers of the very popular 1-2-3 spreadsheet, had announced Symphony, another entry in the integrated PC software field.

Two years after the VisiOn breakthrough at Comdex 1982, Windows was in a rut. Editors had begun to wonder in print about whether Windows would ever actually be ready. Despite all the Windows doom and gloom, Microsoft's other markets prospered. Fiscal 1984 revenues neared $100 million, spurred by old standby BASIC's continued success, while the Microsoft corporation now tallied more than 600 employees.

The Windows project seemed to have taken on a life of its own. Microsoft explained away delays but these very delays resulted in higher expectations of the final product. Finally, on November 20, 1985, Microsoft shipped the eagerly anticipated Windows to dealers and distributors. To quell the inevitable backlash from critics who had waited so long, Microsoft held a "Windows Roast," where Gates and Ballmer joined with industry analysts to poke fun at themselves and Windows' many traumas. With true PR savvy, Gates not only managed to generate more fanfare for Windows but also co-opted the existing industry criticism and aggravation as his own.

By the end of 1985, Microsoft was generating a pretax profit margin greater than 34 percent with $38 million in the bank and no debt. Finances were not a problem. With a generous employee stock option plan, by 1987 Microsoft would reach 500 shareholders, the point when the SEC requires that a company go public.

Despite the pressing concerns of Windows, the Microsoft Excel spreadsheet and myriad other items, Gates decided to take the company public before being forced to by the SEC. Putting everything else on hold, Salesman Bill took off (the ever-penurious chairman flying coach, of course), drumming up support for the IPO on a 10-day, 8-city whirlwind tour.

Microsoft stock hit the exchange floor on March 13, 1986, to a ravenous pack of Microsoft-hungry wolves. By day's end the stock had run from an opening price of $21 up to $27.50 at the closing bell. Gates made $1.7 million on the stock he sold while retaining shares worth $311 million. All in a day's work, of course.

CLASH OF TITANS

In June 1985 Microsoft and IBM updated their relationship with the Joint Development Agreement stipulating that the two companies would work together to develop an updated version of DOS, entitled DOS 5. It was, according to Gates, "by far the biggest contract we've ever signed." Not surprisingly, a culture clash ensued.

To the Microsoft code writers who thought of themselves as programming artists, the more compact the code, the better. IBM's code quotas, on the other hand, encouraged programmers to write as many lines of code as possible per day. To the Microsofties this was pure insanity. There were other conflicts between the "suits" at IBM and Microsoft's hard-core types as well, all of which led, in 1989, to a chasm too wide to cross. Up until that time, Ballmer had felt that IBM had to be mollified. Whatever it took to "Get the business, get the business." His concept was simple: When you dance with a bear, the bear leads.

Meanwhile Gates continued to be a tireless pitchman for Windows. In an industry where winners are determined by who makes the fewest mistakes, Microsoft was only slowly pulling away from the competition. Despite initial praise upon its release, bugs

action PLAN

1 Take the road less traveled. Bill Gates was a college dropout and seldom looked the part of a corporate VIP. For extraordinary results, try an extraordinary approach. How will you swim against the tide when you sell and serve?

2 Tailor your approach to your buyer. When Gates applied to Harvard, Yale and Princeton, he presented a different version of himself to each and got in to all three. How will you change your presentations to suit each of your prospects?

3 Get connected. Gates knew that doing business with IBM could only make Microsoft stronger. What's your strategy for developing and maintaining relationships with important customers and business contacts?

4 Know your competitors. To keep pace with the rapidly changing software industry, Gates knew he could lead the competition or be left behind. How will you get more information on your competitors and use it to improve your sales strategy?

had cropped up and there were still few applications short of Microsoft's own Excel spreadsheet written for Windows. As Windows gained converts and became a more valuable commodity, however, Gates seized the advantage, playing hardball with any hardware suppliers who considered other platforms.

Using DOS as a lever, Microsoft gave preferential treatment to customers who followed Microsoft's lead. In effect, Gates was slowly building Microsoft into a dancing bear of his own, filling up his dance card as he jitterbugged across the market.

Some resented the new Microsoft bear, and even took to the courts to drop Microsoft down a notch. On St. Patrick's Day, 1988, Apple Computer sued Microsoft, saying Windows' appearance illegally infringed on Apple's copyrights to the Macintosh's visual displays and images. The suit would drag on for more than four years and eventually cost Microsoft – according to Gates – $9 million and 30 man-years of lawyers. On April 14, 1992, San Francisco District Court Judge Vaughn Walker would rule in Microsoft's favor that Windows did not infringe on the Macintosh copyright.

As competition within the software industry grows and margins shrink, Gates expects that in five years Microsoft's consumer division will bypass business software and languages to become the firm's largest division. Cramming a wealth of information onto a multimedia CD-ROM, the consumer division currently offers everything from encyclopedias to a Jurassic Park-like visual tour through the world of dinosaurs. One day Gates hopes that Microsoft, through a fiber optic network of telephones, faxes, photocopiers, televisions, printers and "personal digital assistants," will provide the solution to any possible end user information need.

When this happens, and Gates is quite confident it will, the challenge will be to help customers dance through the virtual sea of data to find the specific bits of information they need. This, however, is a software question. And when it comes to software, no one dances better than Gates. ▣

Bill Gates is a master salesman. He knows how to adapt to both the market and the competition. He maintains a razor-sharp selling edge at all times and never wavers in his creativity and concentrated effort. How do your sales efforts stack up against this master? Take the benchmark test below:

⑤=Always, ④=Often, ③=Sometimes, ②=Rarely, ①=Never

1. Do you identify specific ways your product will benefit your client?

    ⑤   ④   ③   ②   ①

2. Do you realize that customers buy for their reasons and not yours?

    ⑤   ④   ③   ②   ①

3. Do you consider how changes in your industry or related industries will impact your business?

    ⑤   ④   ③   ②   ①

4. Do you adapt your presentations to highlight other products or services that your company offers?

    ⑤   ④   ③   ②   ①

5. Do you fulfill and then exceed your promises to customers?

    ⑤   ④   ③   ②   ①

6. Does tough competition spur you on to greater creativity?

    ⑤   ④   ③   ②   ①

Your Total _____

Your Final Score Add your score for each question to get your final score. If you scored:

From 25 to 30 points: Congratulations, you are confidently advancing to higher levels of success.

From 18 to 25 points: lYour score indicates you can benefit from changing some of your success habits. Identify the areas where you need improvement and develop a new success plan.

Below 18 points: Develop a daily and weekly plan for success and retake this test every week. With a little more effort and commitment you'll enjoy the benefits of continuous improvement.

TEAM UP WITH COACHING LEGEND

LOU HOLTZ AND LEARN TO OVERCOME ADVERSITY,

SET GOALS AND SELL MORE BY DOING RIGHT.

PHOTO BY WILLIAM COUPON/GAMMA LIAISON

Lou Holtz

Lou Holtz has made a career of sticking to traditional values – hard work, integrity, teamwork, practice and positive thinking – and his career has never looked better. In the years since he began coaching the game he loves, he has seen football become an arena of greed and scandal. Holtz has kept his head clear and his team clean by focusing on goals and achievements. Although not an easy task, his dedication to tough discipline and hard work has paid off for Notre Dame on the field and off. If the measure of a good manager is the success of his or her team members, then Lou Holtz has much to teach managers in any field. Lou Holtz's newest motivational video, *Do Right!*, is now the number-one bestselling video in the corporate market-place. In this *SP* exclusive cover story, Holtz shares his basic rules for living right and doing right.

fascinating fact

Lou Holtz graduated 234th in his high school class of 278.

Lou Holtz had hit rock bottom. Just one season after moving to Columbia, South Carolina, to be assistant coach at USC, the entire staff was fired. Overnight, Holtz found himself unemployed and questioning whether he was in the right profession. He had no money in the bank, had just bought a home, and his wife, Beth, was expecting their third child. Holtz was full of despair. In an effort to lift his spirits, Beth gave him a motivational book on setting goals.

Holtz sat down at the dining room table, let his imagination go, and before he knew it, had drawn up a list of 107 goals he wanted to achieve in his life. Beth looked over the list and suggested one more – find a job.

This favorite anecdote of Lou Holtz's contains several of his basic principles for success. And if anyone is familiar with success, it's the University of Notre Dame's head football coach. In his 30-year career, Holtz has never inherited a winning team, yet has led every one of his teams to a bowl game by no later than the second season.

Out of that experience, he has developed a philosophy of living and winning. You must set goals and they must be goals that are valuable to you personally. Whether you're in the sports arena or the sales arena, says Holtz, setting goals, striving to meet those goals and meeting adversity with a positive attitude are key elements to achieving success.

How you pursue those goals determines the quality of your success. The message that Holtz delivers, both on and off the football field, involves these three principles: do right, do the best you can, and treat others as you'd like to be treated. It's a simple formula that works.

Clearly, the world of business couldn't agree more. Holtz's inspirational video *Do Right!* has become the biggest-selling corporate motivational video in the country. In Lou Holtz, people from all walks of life, and in all stages of their professional lives, have found a voice to listen to.

"To me, success is when you have an objective – any objective – and you pursue it successfully. In other words, you culminate it and get the desired result that you had hoped for," says Holtz. "Success isn't money, it isn't wealth, it's whatever you desire. When you say, 'Hey, this is what's important to me in my life and this is what I'd like to do with my life, and this is the result I would like my efforts to produce,' and when your efforts produce that result, then I think you're successful."

GOAL MAN

If setting goals and achieving those goals are a measure of success, then Holtz positively embodies the word. Of the 107 goals he listed back in 1967 at the lowest point in his life, Holtz has achieved 89, including skydiving and landing on an aircraft carrier.

Two achievements tie for first place as his highest professional moment: when he was named head coach at Notre Dame in 1986, and when he was

Coach Holtz on managing different personalities When asked what advice he would give to managers who are faced day after day with the problems of directing, motivating and controlling salespeople, Coach Holtz shared these thoughts.

The Three Rules: "As I said one day, I don't motivate people real well but I do a great job of eliminating those who aren't motivated. I think you just have to say, this is what we want to do and these are the three rules, and this is what we're gonna operate by. I've got to make sure I'm committed, but if somebody else isn't I'll call him in and say, 'We have an agreement, this is the way it's gonna be and I don't believe you're doing the best you can and I wanna know why.' Or, 'I don't think that's the way you'd like to be treated.'

achievement LESSONS

"You just have those three rules and then be very, very confident that if you follow those three rules you're going to get things done. If you care about people, if you're enthusiastic, if you want to achieve success, you work on developing that, and make that the guidebook you work from. There's just a lot of trust and commitment. That's what's worked for us.

"Everybody's different, and how you approach them may be different, but I think the basic rules and the basic philosophy are the same."

The "Star": "It would be the greatest disservice to allow a "star" to leave here thinkin' that he doesn't need any help. I really do think that'd be doing that guy a tremendous disservice because he's going to find out in this world that you cannot exist alone. You have to be able to get along with people, and I wanna tell you, you've got to be able to get along and communicate with people of all nationalities, backgrounds, intelligence levels, educational backgrounds. You've got to be able to get along with people and you have to rely upon other people.

"Notre Dame has been outstanding for years and yet coaches come and coaches go, and athletes come and athletes go. We do not run a Star-type thing. People make stars out of you, you don't make a star out of yourself."

The "Up and Down" performer: "I have no patience with him. That's the commitment to be the best you can be. Not looking at the scoreboard, not 'I feel good today, I'm going to play well; I don't feel good today, I'm not gonna do well. The game is on TV, and I'm all excited; it's not on TV, I'm not excited.' Our policy is, we're going to be the best we can be in whatever we do and take pride in doing it to the best of our ability."

The "Go-Gettem" starter who fades: "They don't run out of steam, they've just lost sight of the objectives, the motivation. Most people that will quit or hang it up or fade are those that don't believe they're going to be successful in the first place. They start out hoping they can be successful, but when they find out they aren't gonna be by the end of their career, they say, 'Hey, I'm not gonna make it,' so then they develop an attitude, 'Well, I don't care' so that it doesn't look like they failed. It's just they didn't try."

The "Great Individualist": "Usually, the individualist isn't going to be on a great football team or basketball team, or whatever else the case may be. I think the only reason for playing a team sport is because of the relationship you can develop with your other players. If you want to be an individualist, go pick up a golf club or a tennis racquet. Football is a team game in every sense of the word, and that's the only way it can be a worthwhile experience for everybody."

named Coach of the Year in 1988 by United Press International, the Football Writers Association of America, *The Sporting News* and *Football News*.

Holtz recognizes that some goals are "wishes" that he won't achieve. "Sometimes things don't always fall into place. I really wanted to be a scratch golfer, I'm not gonna be a scratch golfer. I'm not going to play a week in Las Vegas as a comedian. There are some things I'm just not gonna be able to do," he chuckles.

Goals can be misguided – putting too much emphasis on money or fame – but Coach Holtz strongly denies critics' complaints that our society is too goal oriented: "If anything, it's under-goal-oriented, and if we do have a problem with the future, it will be because we don't have goals. Without goals, we lose complete motivation."

He also believes that goals make a challenge of life. And he practices what he preaches: "I am a great believer that you should be a participant in life. Don't be a spectator. The worst thing in the world is to go along and watch life happen. Why'd I jump out of an airplane? Because I wanted to participate in life – I wanted to know what it was like. I've gone on a submarine, landed on an aircraft carrier, had dinner at the White House."

And your successes – goals achieved – keep paying dividends: "You know, you do something one time, you live it a thousand times. I never go up in an airplane that I don't look out and think, 'I'll betcha we're at 10,000 feet now,' because that's what it looked like when I jumped."

For a person whose achievements are measured by others in wins and losses, it's no surprise that "winning" is a goal to Lou Holtz. But everyone's goals can't be listed in won-lost columns.

"The key word to remember is 'Win,' W-I-N, which stands for 'What's Important Now.' You decide what you want to do, you say 'What's Important Now.' When my children go to college, I tell them, just put this by your bed, 'WIN, what's important now.' I better get up and go to class. I want to graduate, that's what I've got to do now. You know, it looks like it may be four years off but if you just focus on what you have to do, then pretty soon those things will become a reality."

STUMBLES AND FUMBLES

Holtz bristles at the suggestion that successful people are just plain lucky, noting two of the lowest points in his professional life – in 1967 after he'd been fired at the University of South Carolina and later in 1977, when he resigned as head coach of the New York Jets after just one season.

"There's nobody that's ever been successful who hasn't had adversity, or had problems. I think that's what really separates the successful persons from the unsuccessful ones. The successful person will not get discouraged when he faces adversity, because you're going to have it," insists Holtz.

"There's always a tendency to say, 'Well, gee, he's successful, boy, everything went right.' It doesn't work that way. It's a constant altering, adjusting and understanding that you're gonna have adversity and problems." Holtz teaches his players that they must get up from every tackle, every block, determined to win the next encounter.

> ## fascinating fact
>
> *Lou Holtz is a skilled amateur magician.*

"I can honestly say, from the bottom of my heart, I have never had a crisis in my life or a setback that's not made me stronger, and it's turned out to be a positive thing in my life – if I reacted positively to it. And many times I feel that the adversity and the setbacks that you experience are preparing you for something bigger and better, so when you get in that situation, or even a tougher one in the future, you'll be able to handle it."

Holtz is the first to admit that picking yourself up after a setback is painful – and it doesn't happen overnight.

"You don't always turn adversity around immediately. You don't wake up the next day and everything's fine. There's a certain mourning period that we're all gonna go through. I think that's natural. It's hard to get through it, but you aren't going to be able to go through this world without pain.

"To make steel you have to go through fire, and the same thing is true in life. It would be great if you never had any pain or disappointment or if everything went exactly your way, but that isn't the way life is meant to be. It's the attitude we have and how we approach life that's going to determine whether we're going to be happy."

action PLAN

1 Be a goal-getter. When the chips were down in 1967, Lou Holtz started setting goals to get his life back on track. You need goals both to get motivated and to chart your progress. What goals are you currently working toward and what new ones will you set when you reach them?

2 Rise above adversity. "I have never had a crisis in my life or a setback that's not made me stronger," says Holtz. When winners stumble or fall, they get back up and keep going. The next time you're faced with a dilemma or disappointment, what will you do to overcome it and learn from it?

3 Follow the Golden Rule. Doing right by others, says Holtz, helps you win the game of life. To be successful as a person and salesperson, you treat others as you want to be treated. How can you be more sensitive to the wants and needs of others and set your own needs aside to take care of theirs?

DOING RIGHT

Long before Spike Lee coined the film phrase "Do the Right Thing," Lou Holtz was living proof that doing right pays off. "I'm not a philosopher and I'm not preachin' or anything else, I just know this: If I don't do what's right in my heart – and I don't always do it – I'm going to pay a price for it somewhere along the line."

Holtz applies the rule to his own life. "I know when our football squad reports in the fall they're going to want to know, 'Has Coach made the necessary preparations?' because if I haven't, I certainly can't ask them to do it.

"Whenever I have a difficult decision to make, I ask myself, 'What's the right thing to do?' You know, if you do what's right, it'll usually come out. If I have a disagreement with a clerk or a store, you know how we always have disagreements, I just say, 'Well, what do you think is the right thing here?' I'll tell you what, it saves a lot of arguments!"

He also believes it's fair to expect others to "Do the right thing." "If an individual is violating the rules and winning illegally, I feel it's a right and fair and honest thing to report that individual. Not to hurt him or anything else but, you know, there are certain rules that we have to go by. Now if, if I can't do that very, very graciously I will just go along with it. This race is a long one, maybe he's winning today, maybe he looks like he's on top, but I guarantee you this, the person that doesn't do what he feels is right deep down inside is going to be a very miserable, unhappy individual regardless of what he portrays to you.

"I'm only held accountable for my actions and I

want to make sure that my actions are the right and proper ones. I can't account for what other people do, or do to me, but if I've got to live the way he does in order to get on top then I don't want to be on top. That's my belief."

Notre Dame has the greatest following of any football team in America, and thousands of these fans have never been to South Bend. Lou Holtz identifies with these fans and they identify with him.

"I think people can identify with me because I'm a blue-collar person, who's just a plain, simple individual and that's all I am. I'm not smart, I'm not tall, I'm not impressive looking, I've got a lisp, I wear glasses. I was born in a two-room cellar. I think that people can look and say, 'I can identify with him. Here is an average individual – at best – who happens to be at Notre Dame, and what he's saying, he really and truly believes in.'"

Not surprisingly, the modest Holtz admits he really didn't want to make the bestselling video *Do Right*.

"I don't go and say I want to make videos and I want to make speeches. I make speeches because I have a message that I believe in and if I can share it, maybe I can make a difference in somebody's life. I think I have, but only because I can say here's an average person and man, there isn't anything special about him, and I feel that.

"A lot of people have influenced me. I don't think you can be around anybody that's not going to influence you. The only difference between you now and where you're going to be five years from now are the people you meet and the books you read. And reading books and the people I've met, they've all influenced me."

faScinating fact

Holtz graduated from Kent State University in 1959 with a B.A. in history.

Becoming head coach at Notre Dame has been Lou Holtz's greatest personal achievement, but it is clearly not the end of his pursuit of goals. Tomorrow always offers another opportunity to learn, to grow, to succeed.

"As long as I can contribute to this institution then I would love to stay here, but things change, people change, times change. That's the one thing that all businesses have to remember, that people change and these changes, you've got to be able to adjust to them. My health: You know, I'm in good physical health right now, but if all of a sudden I'm tired and I'm worn out and I'm exhausted and I'm irritable and I lose enthusiasm to coach and to put forth the effort it takes, then I'd be totally unfair to Notre Dame to stay here. I think you have that obligation to yourself, your family, your occupation and, in my case, to the University of Notre Dame." ▣

Lou Holtz knew that winning seasons depended on his own positive outlook and how much fight he put into the Fighting Irish. To reach bowl games and win national championships, Holtz practiced the "do right, do your best and follow the Golden Rule" advice that he preached. With this quiz you can find out if you and Holtz have a great attitude in common and how you can weave his best qualities into a tapestry of success.

⑤=**Always,** ④=**Often,** ③=**Sometimes,** ②=**Rarely,** ①=**Never**

1. I tend to view problems as temporary challenges and face them with a positive attitude and a plan of action.

    ⑤   ④   ③   ②   ①

2. I approach each day knowing what my priorities are (What's Important Now) and work accordingly.

    ⑤   ④   ③   ②   ①

3. I observe other salespeople in action and try to make their best techniques part of my own strategy.

    ⑤   ④   ③   ②   ①

4. I set goals not only for my sales and professional success, but in nonwork-related areas as well.

    ⑤   ④   ③   ②   ①

5. I understand that disappointments are inevitable, and prepare myself to deal with them without being pessimistic.

    ⑤   ④   ③   ②   ①

6. I always make an effort to do right, do my best and follow the Golden Rule.

    ⑤   ④   ③   ②   ①

Your Total _____

Your Final Score Add your score for each question to get your final score. If you scored:

From 25 to 30 points: Lou Holtz would welcome you to his team. Since you often get back what you give away, why not become a coach to someone else and help that person develop your skills and attitude. The day may come when they return the favor, but you win no matter what.

From 18 to 25 points: If you expect too much too soon, your discouragement may show up in your sales. For each three or below you scored, give yourself time to make a positive change in that area. Choose someone you work with who excels in that area as a role model, and record your improvements in a journal to track your progress.

Below 18 points: If you're going to make the cut, you have to make it happen. Skills are only half of the equation — you'll also need the right attitude to rise to the top. Decide what goals you want to achieve, then work on your preparation and organization skills so you have a specific plan for reaching them. If you don't already know what's important now, figure out which activities improve your sales most and stick to those.

HOW JACKIE JOYNER-KERSEE MANAGES

HER TIME, TALENT AND THOUGHTS TO

MAINTAIN A LONG-LASTING WINNING STREAK.

PHOTO BY PAUL J. SUTTON/DUOMO

Jackie Joyner-Kersee

Known as the greatest living female athlete, she runs like a gazelle, jumps like a leopard and speaks with the soft assurance of a woman who knows the peace of victory won fair and square. Talent alone does not make a champion and Jackie Joyner-Kersee credits solid hometown roots, close family values, the help of friends and fans along the way, her trainer husband Bob Kersee and her own indomitable spirit for propelling her to the top in grueling competitions that chew up younger women. In fact, Kersee has outlasted most of her early competition and continues to outdistance the younger challengers. In an exclusive interview with *SP*, Jackie Joyner-Kersee shares her reasons for continuing in competition and her secrets for staying at the very top of her form.

Although this one-woman Olympic powerhouse grew up in a town of burned-out homes, abandoned housing projects, vacant factory shells and railroad yards that had long ago succumbed to nature's scruffier side, she nevertheless found the momentum and drive to pick her life up and make it fly. Kersee, along with many other hopeful young athletes, met up with Coach Nino Fennoy who has sent more than 50 young athletic stars from Lincoln High School in Kersee's hometown of East St. Louis, Illinois, off to college on track scholarships.

fascinating fact

Jackie Joyner-Kersee was named for Jacqueline Kennedy, who was first lady when Joyner-Kersee was born.

Kersee, who attended UCLA on a basketball scholarship, took that leg up and went quite a few better. In 1989 she returned triumphant from Seoul's Olympic Games with gold medals in both the heptathlon (in which she recorded a world record of 7,291 points) and the women's long jump (an Olympic record of 24 ft., 3.5 in.).

GROWING UP FAST

Looking back, Kersee candidly admits that times as a youngster were tough but that she never looked at her family's situation as hopeless or helpless. "Getting through the struggle is the reason I am here today," she states.

Her high school track and field coach remembers Kersee as just one of the pack until her 13th birthday when a light seemed to shine from within and it was Jackie's turn to make her move. She hasn't stopped since.

> **fascinating fact**
>
> *Jackie Joyner-Kersee could leap 17 feet by the time she was 12 years old.*

"I think for me it was talent and the desire to do better. I could tell in practice each day I was getting better and learning more. Each time I would go to a competition was my chance to challenge what I had done," Kersee says.

She wasn't competing against her last best effort, explains Kersee, but running better with proper mechanics. "Doing something properly is the most important for me," she explains, "because at some time I'm going to run against somebody who's as talented as I am."

In that situation, according to Kersee, the person who makes the least amount of mistakes usually is going to come out on top. "You can be talented, but if you lack the discipline that it takes to be the best, you won't win," she adds.

It's a matter of balancing each effort and disciplining yourself within that balance. In the scant minute before an athlete hits the runway for the jump, Kersee claims that the time whizzes by. "If you see the red light you are disqualified. But that minute goes so fast and the interesting thing is the pressure. The world may be watching but it comes down to you and God."

Jackie Joyner-Kersee's Championship Management Strategies

1. Manage your time: Use the time you have away from your areas of professional pursuit to develop yourself as a person, to enlarge your interests, to think creatively, to plan for reaching your goals.

2. Manage your body: Eat healthy foods, get enough rest, take time for yourself, exercise regularly. By maintaining a healthy physical standard you build in a high resistance to stress, a can-do feeling that carries you through the tough times.

achievement LESSONS

3. Manage your thought patterns: Feed your mind with useful information. Use thoughts as active facilitators to engage your body in activities that will further or enhance your goals. Use your thoughts for positive reinforcement and powerful expectations.

4. Manage your commitments: Realize that you can't be all things to all people all the time. Mark out blocks of time for your own commitments to yourself. Follow a predictable pattern of activities outside of your stated goals.

VISIONS OF GOLD

Kersee says she does not become a passive activator nor an observer from outside herself. In fact, she takes an active facilitating role, seeing herself go through every motion in exactly the right sequence.

"Before I go down the runway, I visualize what I want to do. At the Olympic Games they have monitors. You can see your previous jump and see what you're doing wrong. I went back and visualized what I was supposed to do correctly and then I was able to do it. I have always been able to visualize and then put that into action. I think it comes from being prepared," she reasons.

Rather than watching a film of herself in her own head, Kersee says she sees the successful outcome of her own actions in present time.

"I visualize myself being successful. I see it and it's up to me to perform it. Once I'm standing there, I see myself running down the runway. I see myself kicking off. I see myself jumping. I see myself landing. I see myself coming off the pit. What an excellent jump! I see all of that. Now it's time for me to do it. As I'm running down the runway, I'm only feeling it. I'm not seeing it anymore. And everything happens just like I saw it."

What Kersee describes for one event she practices for many. It's an astounding record of multiple accomplishment and dedication to discipline.

"I can feel the movements that I visualize," she says. "I really can feel myself. Once I visualize it and it's time to go, I feel that. It's tough at times, because when you're trying to achieve something, sometimes things distract you, things get in the way and keep you from going through your regular routine. And for some reason or another, the most important time of your career, especially for me in the Olympic Games, there were so many distractions and there I was trying to concentrate. That's where you really have to find that quiet time for concentration."

Kersee admits that all the Olympic competitors had the same distractions, but for the person picked to win, it was tougher.

Says Kersee, "I kept telling myself not to worry about the gold medal. I had to concentrate on what I had to do and that was performing very well.

"I thrive on the competition. Sometimes it's difficult to be up all the time at practice. Practice is harder than competition. You do more repeats. Competition is one race and that's it. I know that even though I'm the record holder there is someone out there working to try to beat me. So that's in the back of my mind."

GETTING BETTER WITH AGE

At 28 Kersee should be hitting her stride. "I'm looking to go through '93 because for track and field athletes you really start in your prime around 28. If you look at some of our top women athletes their best times have come when they were actually 29 or 30 years of age. I think that's a combination of taking care of your body and making sure that you're getting proper rest. I have not done any research on this but that is the conclusion that I have come up with from the people that I have seen and watched. But I have not put a limit on when I want to stop because I believe that once you start to put limitations on whatever it is you want to do you never reach the goal that you set out to meet. My goal is the World Championships in Tokyo and next it's the Olympic Games."

By taking it one year at a time and setting realistic goals for the future, Kersee has carved out a mega-career that begins with her commitment to solid values and family life.

"I try to take it one year at a time and realize that year is going to be tougher than the previous year," she explains. When accused of using steroids she quietly but vehemently denied it. When the press tried to cook up a competition between herself and her equally successful sister-in-law, Florence Joyner, Kersee calmly explained that blood is thicker than medals. Although she has been hurt by media attacks, she has grown to withstand them and has moved ever forward in her quest for competitive brilliance.

When asked if it's lonely at the top, the way people say it is, Kersee simply replies, "Yes. It's tough being on the top. You have to keep everything in perspective. You have to understand that this is something you worked for and now that you are there you have to continue to work hard to stay there. And for me, that brings me back to a challenge. At one point, someone else was on top and I was targeting for that position. And now that I have that position, I have to continue to remember that regardless of where I am at this time, there is always someone there working to take the spot from me. So I have to constantly understand...I don't have time to relax. I have to work hard and understand that the goals that I have set forth are not easy goals to attain. So if I'm working hard and trying to reach those goals, someone else is trying to reach those same goals."

RUNNING ON EMPTY

In Kersee's arena, success and second best is measured in a hundredth of a second. That's tough pressure.

"I learned a lot about myself in 1984," Kersee reveals. "I was 21. It was my first Olympic Games. I was picked to win the gold medal. Mentally, I wasn't ready.

action PLAN

1 Polish your technique. The stronger your skills, the better your results. "Doing something properly is the most important for me," says Kersee, and it should be for you as well. What can you do to keep your prospecting, closing and other selling skills up to par to maximize your performance?

2 Get tough on yourself. For those times when you'd rather be playing, self-discipline keeps you working. As Kersee says, "If you lack the discipline it takes to be the best you won't win." How can you motivate yourself to make the calls, keep the appointments and do all the other things you must do to succeed, even when you don't feel like doing them?

3 Manage your time. With more time to make calls, you stand to earn more sales. Kersee manages her time carefully to fit the things she wants to do into her schedule, and by using your time wisely as well, you can reduce stress and increase sales. What can you do to be more aware of how you spend your time and learn to use it more efficiently?

Physically, I was. I had a hamstring problem which a lot of people think was the reason I didn't win. But that's not true. When I went to the line, I was thinking about the injury. I kept feeding myself negative thoughts. Not once did I go to that line thinking I was the champion. I was very hesitant in attacking the hurdles. I was intimidated by the high jump. And through the two-day competition I hung in there, but mentally I drained myself completely.

fascinating fact

In 1986, Jackie Joyner-Kersee set two world records in 26 days.

I didn't even replenish my fluids. I was just drained. When it came down to the last event – the 100 meter – I had to stay within a half second or a second with the other girl, and I didn't do that because coming down the stretch of the last 100 meters I was just totally exhausted. And I ended up losing the gold medal by five points."

Her exhaustion, she feels, was almost totally self-induced. "I honestly believe that if you continue to tell yourself something, eventually your body starts reacting to the things that you've told it," Kersee says. "In the 1984 Olympic Games, I kept saying to myself, 'This leg is not going to hold up.' And I wouldn't eat. And it's important for me to eat between events because with two-day competition we're out there all day and I lose anywhere from 8 to 10 pounds. Then without eating, I don't know how much weight I have lost. I was fragile and I lost muscle mass."

STRICT SELF-MANAGEMENT

Of the two essential management concepts – time management and self-management – managing her body and the mind that tells that body what it should have is up to her. She shares setting up healthful and motivating regimens with coach/husband Bob Kersee who also coaches the UCLA track team.

"My husband Bobby and I try to go 50/50 but it doesn't always work out that way. In time management and self-management it still comes down to self-discipline. Bobby might tell me this is important for me to do, but if I don't have enough discipline to do it, I'm going to suffer in the long run. For instance, this year we decided I shouldn't compete indoors because I was dedicating a lot of time to doing work with Team Xerox. So we put me on a timetable that means at certain times of the year I'm going to cut off all personal appearances. Self-management comes in when I know it's time to cut out all the junk foods and potato chips. Bobby suggests to all of us that it is important to start eating carbohydrates and pasta and all these things. But it is up to us to have the self-discipline to do it," Kersee explains.

During training Kersee and the rest of the team are on the track at 7:30 a.m. They walk for a mile, then run another mile. Then it's into the weight room to do weight training. They leave UCLA around 10:30 a.m. and from 11 to 4 they occupy their time with something other than television – either reading a book or doing some other work. At 4:00 p.m. they return to the track to do the same warm-up and some interval work which will last for approximately two hours. At about 6:00 p.m. the team leaves UCLA for an evening without television from 8 to 10, except for news watching.

"We sat down and talked about this regimen and Bobby said he was not going to watch everybody. This is where self-discipline comes in. At first I didn't agree with him. I didn't think it was right for him to say we couldn't watch TV," Kersee remembers. "Now I think it's pretty good. It all comes down to managing your time efficiently by doing worthwhile things. Every Thursday morning we would sit down and talk about what we were doing with that time. And I learned that it allowed me a lot of time to come up with creative ideas for a presentation that I might be planning on doing in the future."

Kersee found that actively managing her time also allowed for a certain ordered approach to making herself a more balanced person outside of athletics. Now she thinks about blocks of time and how to use them efficiently and effectively to move toward her goal.

KERSEE CAUSES

When Kersee takes to the road for speeches or promotional tours, heads naturally turn. Although she has had her share of hurtful press, she remains courteous, sensitive and generous with her time.

When somebody says or prints something about Kersee that she knows is false, she says simply, "I've learned to realize that eventually those in the dark will come to the light. Regardless of whether someone said something negative or derogatory, I don't feel it is my place to compound it by trying to say, 'That's not right.' I look beyond that because sometimes people have hidden agendas. Sometimes reporters come to a press conference with the idea that they're going to write a particular story. I just don't let it get to me. Especially after '88 with the drug issue. That was tough. It wasn't as bad for me as it was for some others like my sister-in-law – they came down harder on her. You can deny, and deny, and deny, and deny but when people's minds are already made up, I have to let my record speak for itself."

Along with a grueling training schedule, Kersee spends much of her time appearing on behalf of causes, many of them related to young people in school.

"If I think it is a wonderful cause, I'll do it," she states matter-of-factly. "I have to weigh all the requests to look at how much I have done so far. I have to find a proper place to train and make sure that I continue to work out. If it's going to take away from my training, I have to consider it very carefully. I have to prioritize activities that are outside of training. Things will come in like Black History Month, Career Day and things like that, that I think are important. When kids are involved and I can do something in the community then I will commit to doing it.

"There are certain times of the year like April and May that I will only do one appearance because those are important months for me to train. June is the Nationals. Then I will set up a lot of things for August after the World Championships are over. It's hard trying to convey this to people because they think you just go out and run."

In managing a successful sports career, the problem of overload is always there. "Over the years," says Kersee, "one thing we have learned is that you can't grant everybody's wishes. There are times when I don't want to say 'No' but I have to or I'll get burned out. We make sure that I'm doing enough, but also that I'm doing enough with kids. If I could do it all, I would. But I have learned that I can't."

When asked if she ever thought success would be so difficult, Kersee answers with characteristic simplicity: "I don't look at it as being difficult. In all my dreams of going to the Olympics and winning a gold medal, I never realized all the other things that were going to come afterward. It has all been pretty amazing." ▣

When she races she lines up with the rest of the field, but Jackie Joyner-Kersee's discipline, visualization and preparation always give her a head start. To cross the finish line first in sales, you can make the same qualities work for you. Use this quiz to compare your success habits with Kersee's, then make improvements as suggested to stay on track.

⑤=Always, ④=Often, ③=Sometimes, ②=Rarely, ①=Never

1. I use books, videos, role plays and other materials and methods to enhance my selling skills.

   ⑤   ④   ③   ②   ①

2. I exercise self-discipline to finish all the things I know I need to do every day.

   ⑤   ④   ③   ②   ①

3. I keep myself in good physical condition to enhance my sales performance.

   ⑤   ④   ③   ②   ①

4. I manage my time effectively to maximize my productivity.

   ⑤   ④   ③   ②   ①

5. I visualize sales calls and presentations so I know just how I want them to go before I make them.

   ⑤   ④   ③   ②   ①

6. When I need to focus on a task, I am able to ignore distractions.

   ⑤   ④   ③   ②   ①

Your Total _____

Your Final Score Add your score for each question to get your final score. If you scored:

From 25 to 30 points: Way to go — you are taking huge strides toward success. As you keep up the good work, remember that just as Kersee supported her favorite causes in her spare time, you need to balance your sales career with other areas of your life.

From 18 to 25 points: You're doing fairly well, but with a little more self-discipline you can improve. Write down a list of three skills you want to strengthen, then work with your manager to develop an improvement plan. Follow your plan daily until it becomes a habit, then develop new plans as you recognize the need to strengthen other skills.

Below 18 points: If you always seem short of time, and have trouble focusing and visualizing success, you may lack organizational skills. To organize your mind, start with your desk. Make sure your work area has a place for everything, and put everything in its place. Every day, make a to-do list for the following day so your time is planned in advance. If you continue to have problems, discuss them with your manager.

CNN'S TALK SHOW HOST WITH THE MOST TELLS

HOW TO GET BUYERS TALKING AND BOUNCE

BACK TO THE TOP AFTER YOU HIT ROCK BOTTOM.

PHOTO BY STARR/GAMMA LIAISON

Larry King

Larry King's broadcasting mentor had the word "Salesman" after occupation on his driver's license. King neither peddles policies nor calls on accounts, but he has created a phenomenal success by building rapport while selling people on opening up to him in front of millions of listeners and viewers. From his early days in radio, broadcasting from a hotel lobby in Miami, his reputation has grown until he is now considered one of the giants of communication – with a big "C." Honored by professional societies, feted by celebrities and courted by posh resorts, he nevertheless remains unabashedly excited about what he does best – getting people to talk.

fascinating fact

Larry King was born Lawrence Harvey Zeiger on November 19, 1933.

Someone once said that success in convincing a person to buy your product is a matter of doing a thorough job selling yourself first. If you accept that premise, then you must also admit that Larry King, in his own language, is one helluva salesman. Guest after guest, night after night, month after month, year after year, King has been a consummate professional who knows how to get, and keep, the prospect's attention.

CURIOUS LARRY

Ever since Larry King was eight years old he wanted to talk – and listen – to people. His natural curiosity about people's vocations, avocations, experiences, feelings and talents was boundless. One can easily imagine little Larry, standing beside his mother at the butcher shop, peppering the man in the white apron behind the counter with questions like, "Why rib roast? What's it like being a butcher? Do women come in here and tell you their problems? Didja ever want to go into vegetables?"

After 30 years in broadcasting, Larry King, who is listed in *The Guinness Book Of World Records* as having logged more hours on national radio than any other talk show host, estimates that he has interviewed more than 30,000 people. Numbers, however, do not begin to tell the Larry King story of success. Because King – and the name suits – is above all an interviewer who draws people to him while drawing them out. How can one explain why celebrities, politicians, authors, presidents and ex-presidents, athletes and performing artists all feel comfortable and amiable sitting in front of this gregarious and articulate inquisitor? The one quality, above and beyond talent, experience, insight and all the rest appears to be that King is always, on camera or off, natural. He knows who he is, what his weaknesses are and where his strengths lie. He never deviates from what makes him comfortable. He is always himself.

fascinating fact

At the last minute, King escaped military service during the Korean War because of poor vision in one eye.

"As a kid I had an innate curiosity and a love of broadcasting. I always wanted to get into it, first radio, then television. And I was the kind of kid who interviewed everybody I met: 'Why do you drive a bus? What's good about being a cop?' So I'm just extending what I always did. I always thought I would go into sports broadcasting but in retrospect interviewing comes naturally to me. On radio and television, the producers book the guests so I talk to whoever shows up. Since I'm curious about everything, it doesn't matter to me who sits in that chair. In fact, I am very easy to book for. I'm more comfortable ad libbing than if I had something to read. I never read the books people are plugging. If I did, the questions wouldn't be fresh. I'd already know the answers and we'd have to talk about something else."

Getting people to open up is an art which Larry King has mastered. From such press-shy legendary greats as Frank Sinatra to master motivator Zig Ziglar, King elicits the same open confidence and camaraderie. Certain skills, which King claims are absolutely essential to one-on-one rapport, are easily transferable to other professional situations where rapport can be the deciding factor between a make-or-break pitch. One is the attitude King carries into all his interviews – he's impartial. Number two – the guest rates priority number one in any close encounter of the King kind. King never prejudges the guest's point of view. He has no ax to grind or buried bones to unearth. He is committed to letting the guest's light shine.

"There isn't a soul who won't talk to you if you are sincerely interested in them. But you have to create that empathy. The way you do that is you walk in their shoes a little and then you try to find out what those shoes are like. What is it like to step on a stage? What is it like to be known by everybody? What is it like to run a company? Now there is no chief executive officer who doesn't like to tell you about that. You could just as well say, 'Your company lost a lot of money last year – what the hell's wrong?' But confrontation never works for me. Now you always have to do what works for you. What works for me is a little naivete – innocence – even though it is obvious that I know what is going on in the world. Even if I have a guest on the show whose views are contrary to mine – he's the guest."

He reigns supreme over today's talk realm, but Larry King has seen his share of trouble. Still, financial woes and even a heart attack couldn't keep him down. To make sure setbacks don't stop you either, learn these lessons from Larry.

Expect to make mistakes. "Famous people can screw up and so can the host," says King — and so can you. On the fast track to the top, you can expect to stumble now and then. Be prepared for setbacks and you won't be as shaken by them.

Learn from the error. After King went bankrupt, he paid someone else to manage his money. After his heart attack, he quit smoking and changed his diet. Mistakes can be helpful when they effect positive change. Ask yourself what you can learn from your blunders and what you can change to keep them from recurring.

achievement LESSONS

Keep taking your chances. King says that good communicators take risks; risk taking helps salespeople reach new heights as well. Guard against letting disappointments keep you inside your comfort zone. Instead, assess what you stand to gain and lose and take risks without being reckless.

TO BANKRUPTCY AND BACK

It is well known that Larry King has had financial troubles in the past. Even while he was a successful radio show host in Miami, money slipped through his fingers or into bad investments and, in 1973, he declared personal bankruptcy. In his book *Tell It To The King* (Larry King with Peter Occhiogrosso; G. P. Putnam's Sons, NY), he recalls that time. In his pocket he had the remaining half of a round-trip plane ticket from Miami to L.A. where he had gone to seek work at any radio or TV station that would have him. The trip was a washout and, on the last day, with a scant three dollars in his pocket, he stopped his rental car (in those days, as King recalls, you could still rent a car for cash at the airport) at the Beverly Hills Hotel, walked the flight down to the coffee shop and ordered a milkshake to fill up his empty stomach. The check came to three dollars and King was chagrined at not being able to dole out a tip to the countergirl. To get his car from valet parking he made up a story about leaving his wallet behind in his hotel room, drove straight to the airport, used the same line at the car rental return and told them to bill him, then approached a friendly looking fellow in the airport terminal and asked to borrow some money for newspapers to read on the plane. The man gave him five dollars and told him to get a bite to eat and King arrived back in Miami completely broke and still unemployed.

> ### fascinating fact
>
> *Larry Zeiger became Larry King on May 1, 1957, when he went on the air for the first time on Miami's WAHR radio.*

Fourteen years later, Larry King, now famous and successful, arrived at the eighth annual Ace Awards, cable television's highest honor, where he would emcee (for which he was paid five thousand dollars) and where he would also receive the award for best talk-show host. He arrived escorted by Angie Dickinson in her Mercedes and they pulled up to the Beverly Hills Hotel where the luncheon was to be held. Flash bulbs popped, the press crushed toward them, and King found himself on the same stairs leading to the coffee shop, where milkshakes were now four dollars. Dazed for the moment, he looked around and felt strange and at the same time extremely proud. Six weeks later he had a heart attack which resulted in multiple bypass surgery and a new way of life for King.

"My book is about famous people who put their pants on one leg at a time. Famous people can screw up and so can the host. In my case, the two greatest failings were also the two best things that happened for me. Financial failure and heart failure. I couldn't handle money. If I hadn't gotten knocked down, I would have continued borrowing from Peter to pay Paul. I would still be in Miami making $70,000 and spending $90,000. But I got shut down so bad that when I came back, I put the money in other people's hands to manage for me. I have no idea what a CNN or Mutual Broadcasting paycheck looks like. The money all goes to Boston where I pay the management firm $113,000 a year to manage my money. In 1983 I wasn't even making that much in a year. I got real lucky. The CNN show took off. But now I'm still living like I was in 1983 when I was making $100,000 a year and paying the manager in Boston $10,000. It's fine. I have a company Lincoln Continental, I fly first class which is in my contract. When I land there is a limo waiting. The rest is all invested for me. Now I can afford tips. On a recent trip to La Costa I tipped $1,000 on a $4,200 bill. After I declared bankruptcy, I started all over again. I lived with my mother for awhile. I got lucky and went right back on the radio and back to the newspaper. Within two years I had the television talk show. But most of my failures or disappointments were self-inflicted. I can look back and say very few people wronged me. After the heart attack, I changed my lifestyle – no more smoking, I watch my diet now – I lost weight. I have been lucky enough to survive both calamities and come back to feel terrific. I put my financial house in order only because I take care of myself and other people take care of my money for me."

LARRY KING LIVE

Larry King's expertise and charisma as an interviewer is matched by his presence in front of an audience. He delights in holding them in the palm of his hand, leading them to a punch line, developing the drama of a good yarn well spun. He never reads a speech nor does he even know beforehand what particular story he may use to lay his audience in the aisles. All alone, he stands there, he has a sense of whom he is speaking to, and then he lets them have it. From a backlog of stories that goes back to his boyhood in Brooklyn and all the celebrities, politicians, comedians, speakers and tycoons he has known since, he weaves the texture of talk that never fails to rivet the attention of his audience.

"My biggest kick is making people laugh. Interviewing famous people and learning about them is wonderful. But when you can stand up in a room and hear a pin drop, control them and make them laugh, that is the high of all highs. I understand what great comedians go through. That feeling of power that you can go anywhere you want with them. When I would watch comics, before I started doing speeches, I would ask them how they could keep it fresh time after time. They said that every time is like the first time. There is a truism in that because sometimes you are even better because you are so heightened. A warmth develops between you and the audience. I would tell a story and I knew where the ending was and I was as heightened about reaching it as the audience was and I had told it 10 times before. I don't just think of the story on the spot, but I have no idea what stories I will tell or which way it will go when I am up there. A lot depends on the group. So there is a magic."

To the manor born in no way describes King's early life. His father died when Larry was 10. His mother had lost a son before Larry was born and then lost her own mother. Consequently she overindulged Larry and thought he could do no wrong. Life in Brooklyn was poor and it meant street survival for a boy like Larry, which is perhaps why men like Mario Cuomo find in King a comrade in arms and a good friend. King never made the secret vow, "When I grow up I'm going to make it big." Instead, he learned by trial and error that meaning comes before money, and the meaning is what keeps the work rich.

"After my father died we were on welfare for a year. New York City bought my first pair of glasses. My mother spoiled me and that was coupled with the fact that I was never taught much responsibility. On the other hand, she gave me a lot of love. She also gave me an ability to fall down and come up again. Then at 22 I started making $22,000 a year, reading my name in the *Miami Herald* and I wanted to have that Cadillac. But in the beginning, as early as age six I wanted to get on the radio. I never had dreams of a national show. What do you do when reality exceeds your dreams – Albert Brooks says you shut up about it. You stay excited. You stay interested in what makes your guest tick whether you make $10,000 or $1,000,000. The money is a by-product. But in the early days I had too much too soon. Too much attention. I never defined success then. Today I would define it as doing what you want. Phil Donahue told me I made a smart move going with CNN. It was generally printed that CNN gave me $800,000 and I could have gone to ABC for a million-one and to King World for a million-two. Now Donahue told me he makes $3 million. I make $800,000 from CNN and another $400,000 from Mutual so I make a million-two. He can buy a 96-foot yacht, I can buy a 48-foot yacht. I live in a nice apartment, he lives in a nice apartment. But I can put anyone on my show without the network calling me and saying we had a tune-out last night and I've got to put the priest who slept with the goat on tomorrow because it's rating period."

SMOOTH TALKER

In an age when communication has become a catch-all phrase for everything from selling political ideologies to pitching detergent, some super communicators shine like beacons from a lighthouse. Larry King's brief, choppy style keeps the guest and the audience moving along as if on an electric current. Sometimes we get a slight jolt, but more often, we feel the steady surge of juice and we don't want to turn off the switch.

"A good communicator communicates. There are no rules. I don't know why William Faulkner talked in endless sentences when he was a brilliant writer. Arthur Godfrey spoke in a monotone, if you judged his voice alone, but he was a great communicator. Red Barber had a severe Southern twang yet he was great in front of a mike. I am a basic New Yorker who can

action PLAN

1 Create empathy. By putting himself in his guests' shoes, King encourages them to open up to him. To earn your buyers' trust, try to understand what their jobs are like, what pressures and problems they face and how they view you. What can you do to learn more about your buyers and show them you understand them and their situations?

2 Treat prospects with equal courtesy and respect. To bond with guests, King sets his opinion aside and approaches interviews impartially. Valuable prospects don't look, sound or act according to a set formula, so don't prejudge them. How can you stop stereotyping or labeling people and give them all the same courteous, attentive treatment?

3 Tell a tale. King holds audiences spellbound with stories of his boyhood, guests and famous acquaintances. Good stories — especially of someone in circumstances similar to your prospect's — help illustrate your main points, convincing the listener to buy. How can you work more true sales stories into your presentation?

appeal to people in Biloxi. Good communicators take risks. Johnny Carson told me that and it's true. Godfrey was a risk taker. I have nothing prepared before my show and every night I am at risk. I never say to myself, 'Is this a stupid question?' I risk saying, 'I don't know.' I risk going to my instincts and trusting them. I am never dishonest with the audience. For example, I was doing a show in New York and a guy says to me, 'Suppose you were walking down the hall in NBC and a guy grabbed you and sat you down and said Brokaw is sick, here's the news. What would you do?' I told him I would say, 'Good evening ladies and gentlemen. I was walking down the hall, a man handed me a script, told me Tom Brokaw is sick, you're on. I'm Larry King and I have never anchored the news in my life. I am going to read the script. We are going to do the best we can for the next half hour with the *NBC Nightly News*. Bear with me.' Now, what does that accomplish? Nobody tunes out and no screw up can hurt me the whole half hour. They are all with me. That's what Edward Bennett Williams said made a great trial lawyer. Just put one member of the jury in your shoes and you can't lose the case. You may get a hung jury, but you won't lose. Just get one guy to say, 'I understand.'"

The qualities that have helped Larry King survive and thrive in broadcasting are just as useful off the air in one-on-one situations like sales. In fact, King has known some of the great salesmen of our time.

"Gene Letterman, who wrote *The Sale Begins When the Customer Says No,* was fantastic; Harvey Mackay who wrote *How To Swim With The Sharks* was good. Also Herb Cohen, Zig Ziglar, Johnny Carson. You know the truest thing is you sell yourself. Arthur Godfrey was a great salesman. In fact his driver's license said 'Salesman.' He once said to me, 'That's all we are, Larry. I'm just honest enough to put it down.'" ▣

> ## fascinating fact
>
> *Shawn Southwick, 38, is Larry King's seventh wife.*

Larry King didn't grow up with big money or big connections, but he was a winner on the inside. To score your own self-made success, adopt the qualities that helped him talk his way to the top, including curiosity, resilience and empathy. Test yourself to find out if you and King share the same winning characteristics and if not, how to make them part of you and your sales strategy.

⑤=Always, ④=Often, ③=Sometimes, ②=Rarely, ①=Never

1. I try to take a sincere interest in my customers' business problems and in their families and personal interests.

       ⑤   ④   ③   ②   ①

2. I understand my strengths and weaknesses, and make the most of what I have while improving my shortcomings.

       ⑤   ④   ③   ②   ①

3. I try to understand what it's like to be my prospects, and show empathy for their feelings and situation.

       ⑤   ④   ③   ②   ①

4. When I make a mistake, I look for the lesson in it and make positive changes as a result.

       ⑤   ④   ③   ②   ①

5. When buyers are on the fence about my product, I tell a convincing sales story to help them make up their minds.

       ⑤   ④   ③   ②   ①

6. I know taking risks helps me improve, and I'm not afraid to take a chance to earn a new customer.

       ⑤   ④   ③   ②   ①

Your Total _____

Your Final Score: Add your score for each question to get your final score. If you scored:

From 25 to 30 points: Sales records are yours for the breaking. Keep up the good work and keep in mind the meaning of what you do and how it helps others. Someday you may find yourself talking to Larry King in an interview about your phenomenal success.

From 18 to 24 points: You may be losing sight of your buyers' individuality. Remember that they are people, first and foremost. Your curiosity about them, ability to empathize with them and share stories with them tells them you understand that. Spend some extra time with buyers — take them to lunch or just call to make sure they are doing well.

Below 18 points: You probably don't share a strong bond with your buyers and seem easily discouraged by setbacks. Shift your focus from the business to the personal side of selling. When you take care of customers, the numbers may take care of themselves. When you make a mistake or get rejected, objectively analyze the causes, then move on.

THE SUPERSALESMAN FROM MINNESOTA

TELLS THE INSIDE STORY OF HIS BIGGEST SALES.

Harvey Mackay

I t is easy to like and remember Harvey Mackay. Long after you've listened to one of his speeches, and long after you've read his book, his sleek one-liners continue to cruise your mind. "He who burns his bridges better be a damn good swimmer." Or, "It isn't the people you fire who make your life miserable, it's the people you don't." Or, "Find something you love to do and you'll never have to work a day in your life."

Harvey Mackay, owner and CEO of the prosperous Mackay Envelope Corporation in Minneapolis, is a supersalesman. He played a major role in persuading 28 NFL owners to bring the Super Bowl to Minneapolis in 1992, he was a catalyst in getting the $100 million Hubert H. Humphrey Metrodome sports complex built in Minneapolis and he also wrote an international bestseller that made publishing history.

His book *Swim With The Sharks Without Being Eaten Alive* was rated the number-one business book in the United States in 1988 (translated into some 16 languages and distributed in 80 countries). As a result, demand for Mackay – already a popular speaker at major universities like Harvard and Stanford – skyrocketed, making him one of the highest paid speakers in the world today.

> ## fascinating fact
>
> *Mackay Envelope boasts 500 employees and produces 13 million envelopes each day.*

The bottom line? After he received a six-figure advance for the hardcover rights, the paperback rights were sold for a whopping $787,500. In addition, Mackay is reportedly receiving well over $2 million for the publishing rights to his second book, *Beware The Naked Man Who Offers You His Shirt*, subtitled "Love What You Do, Do What You Love, Deliver More Than You Promise," scheduled for release in February 1990.

1. Hungry fighters don't tolerate complacency. Always have your antenna up. Realize that complacency can happen to every single human being. Hungry fighters go to school for a lifetime. We need to use tapes, videos, books and professional magazines to grow. If you don't grow, you die. It's like swimming across a lake. As long as you keep swimming, there is no problem, but as soon as you stop, you're going to go under.

2. Good leadership stretches people. A good leader understands that anything that has been done a particular way for a given amount of time is being done the wrong way. Every single performance can be improved. Look at the field of sports. During the past 20 years every score has improved, regardless of the type of sport. The runners ran faster, the golfing scores went down, the bowling scores went up, high jumpers added inches, tennis balls went faster over the nets, swimmers crossed the finish line faster. Remember the old saying that even if you're on the right track, you'll get run over if you just sit there.

3. Wanting to be number one shouldn't be your number one goal. I never wanted to be the largest envelope manufacturer in the United States. I decided to grow consistently over the past 30 years. I have a high respect for debt and don't want to get carried away by comparing the number of plants or the number of employees. My goal was to get the best return on investment, not to be number one. My mother, a schoolteacher, told me that there would always be somebody with a bigger car, a bigger house, a prettier girl on his arm, but that doesn't matter. Being number one is often laughable. You have to measure yourself by your own standard of performance. You don't even want to try to keep up with the Joneses, because every time you catch up with them, they refinance.

achievement
LESSONS

4. There is no substitute for perfect practice. Practice doesn't make perfect. Perfect practice does. I am not a superior speaker, and I have been speaking for over 15 years, but when I prepared for my book promotions, I took voice lessons to improve my delivery. My voice teacher showed me how to breathe, how to use my voice, how to harness my energy, how to speak without getting hoarse. I am still taking more lessons, I am reading more books on voice training. It is hard work, but there is no substitute for perfect practice. There is also no substitute for the tremendous rewards.

5. Find out what you really want to do. We all have goals, dreams and desires. It's not easy to pin down what you really and truly want out of life. Start writing your dreams and goals on paper. Pale ink is better than the most retentive memory. Then develop identifiable, measurable and attainable goals. Find something that you love to do and you'll never have to work a day in your life.

6. The greatest rewards come from helping other people. My whole philosophy of life is based on personal relationships. That's how I built my company. That's how we got the Super Bowl to Minneapolis, that's how we raised money to build the Metrodome Stadium. One fourth of my time is devoted to volunteerism. I don't do things for people because they can help me. I've raised tens of millions of dollars for all kinds of causes across America, and I don't ever expect one thank-you note. If I expected it, then I'd be in deep trouble and shouldn't be a volunteer. I get the tremendous benefit that comes from the great feeling of helping another person.

When asked how he feels about his chances for producing another bestseller, he responds with a smile, "After a hit, many people lose their intensity, their focus, or they simply stop being as hungry as they were before they wrote the big bestseller. I take pride in challenging myself. I'm a hungry fighter."

SELLING A BESTSELLER

Mackay believes in doing his homework. Before he even wrote his first word, he interviewed more than 100 authors, publishers, agents, lawyers and booksellers. In the process he slowly realized the many obstacles to getting his book published. Harvey explains that publishers receive about 500,000 manuscripts each year, but only 50,000 books get published. That makes the odds of getting published 1 in 10. Once a book is published, the odds of selling the publisher's initial press run of 10,000 books are even lower than that.

During his research Mackay learned that selling books is the only retail business where the merchandise is sold on consignment. The standard industry expression is "gone today and here tomorrow." Unsold books are returned to the publisher's warehouse and then resold at deep discounts. He soon learned that creating a bestseller would be a formidable challenge. Harvey Mackay's creative efforts for meeting this challenge and making it to *The New York Times* bestseller list for more than 52 weeks in a row, provide a unique study in marketing, selling and Midwestern chutzpah.

> **fascinating fact**
>
> Swim With The Sharks Without Being Eaten Alive *spent 54 weeks on* The New York Times *bestseller list.*

"I had to create both an awareness of my book and some competition for it. Fortunately, I was able to talk to a publishing expert who arranged for me to appear live at the Stanford Publishing Program. My manuscript was compulsory reading for a class and I got a unique chance to constructively change the book. At the same time, this session created an opportunity to evaluate my potential for marketing the book."

SELLING THE PUBLISHER

After this eye-opening experience, Mackay went back to the drawing board. He rewrote, polished and edited his manuscript. Then bestselling author Ken Blanchard (*The One-Minute Manager*) arranged a meeting with Larry Hughes, publisher of William Morrow in New York.

"Hughes has a very big and very impressive corner office on Madison Avenue. He also had a key question for me. 'What's so different about your book?' I told him that I had visited at least 100 bookstores and studied the retail business.

"When you walk into a store, you only look at the front covers of the books on display. You see 10 pictures of Iacocca, 10 pictures of Trump. Then I took him to the corner window and asked, 'You see the tops of these trucks? For the past 27 years we have been painting our name, Mackay Envelope Corporation, on the tops of all our trucks which crisscross the United States. There is no significant price difference whether you have two panels or three panels painted.'

"Then I told him to use the same philosophy for selling my book. What's wrong with turning the book around and using the back cover for selling the book? The idea was to use the headline, 'You Can Judge This Book By Its Back Cover,' and display the book twice, the first display showing the front cover, the second display showing the back cover. That way we'd double our chances for selling the book."

GETTING ENDORSEMENTS

The publisher was impressed with Mackay's sales and marketing insights. Later, he was even more impressed when Mackay came back with endorsements from such diverse figures as Ted Koppel, Billy Graham, Gloria Steinem, Walter Mondale and Robert Redford. After a brief negotiation, he agreed to a six-figure advance, a $150,000 advertising and promotion budget and a 100,000-copy first printing. An extraordinarily attractive deal for a first-time author. But how did Mackay get the celebrity endorsements?

"The most important word in the English language, if you want to be a success, can't be found in the dictionary. It's 'Rolodex.'

"I took 48 names and sent these people copies of my book with a nice cover letter. I've met most of these people at one time or another and worked at building the relationship. For example, Ted Koppel came one day to speak at the University of Minnesota. I picked him up at the airport. I knew about his passion for playing tennis and he happened to travel with his tennis racket that day. He thought that there was enough time for hitting a few balls before his speech and we headed for the tennis courts. We had a great time and then raced back to the meeting, with no time to spare. A few days later, I sent him a huge, seven-foot-long, 25-pound tennis racket with an oversize tennis ball and a small poem: 'Here's to the Star of *Nightline*, To help him improve his sightline. Just line up the ball and then whack it, You'll never miss one with this racket.' Ted Koppel sent a note back recommending that I give up poetry. He later sent this endorsement of my book, 'Harvey Mackay takes you on an easy reader ride to success in the business world.'"

DEALING WITH REJECTION

Mackay's contract read that the book title had to be mutually agreeable to both the author and the publisher. William Morrow wanted a different title than *Swim With The Sharks Without Being Eaten Alive*. They told Mackay that the title was too long, that it didn't tell the reader what the book was about, and that some people might think that it was a book about skin diving. After a meeting with the publisher, Mackay's title was voted down 11 to 1. He went back to Minneapolis to rethink his strategy.

"Well, being reasonable, I had to accept the remote possibility that 11 professionals who run one of the most successful publishing houses in America might have a better idea of what would sell in the marketplace. But I wasn't ready to accept it yet. So I went to a local marketing research firm known for their expertise in creating and testing product names for companies like 3M, General Mills or Procter & Gamble. They took 10 people who didn't know anything about business books.

fascinating fact

Mackay is a former number-one ranked tennis player in Minnesota.

They worked on the book title for six hours. During the first hour they had to read about 50 pages of my book. They did not know my title. Their task was to find a title for my business book. After a few hours, they had 800 book titles pasted on the wall of the conference room. Interestingly, one of the titles was *Swim With The Sharks Without Being Eaten Alive*, which someone picked up from a sentence in the text. Then they began to put colored stars next to the titles they liked. Swim With The Sharks... received the most gold stars. Armed with this research, I went back to the publisher and when I left, the vote was 12 to 0 in favor of *Swim With The Sharks*.

SELLING TO THE TOP

In any sales campaign, timing is crucial. The promotion for a book is no different. Harvey learned from publishing experts that the window of opportunity for making the bestseller list consists of a brief, six-week time span immediately following publication. All efforts – advertising, direct mail, media appearances, print interviews, book excerpts in magazines – have to be orchestrated with the precision of a Swiss watch.

"You have to remember that there are 50,000 titles published every year. Every time a book hits the shelves, there are 49,999 titles right behind it, ready to shove it off the shelves, right into the remainder bin. We squeezed a 15-city media tour into a 10-day blur. Publicity included excerpts in the airline magazines, the *Harvard Business Review* and *The Los Angeles Times* with syndication in 40 newspapers across the country. Before the launch, I realized that Waldenbooks, the largest bookselling chain in the country, had ordered only 3,000 books. B. Dalton ordered the same quantity. That meant that *Sharks* would go belly-up before it barely made a splash.

"I went to Stamford, Connecticut, to see Harry Hoffman, chairman of Waldenbooks and one of the most powerful people in publishing and retailing today. It's like going to Mecca, the place is kind of off-limits to authors, and that was all the more reason to go. I told Mr. Hoffman that I was scheduled to go on a 35-city tour and showed him the schedule of 125 radio and TV talk shows across the nation. Once he saw my single-mindedness and commitment, his order went from 3,000 to 15,000 hardcover books. A few days later, B. Dalton did the same. The arch rival across the street had upped the ante."

SELLING AT EVERY LEVEL

At this point, Mackay was ready to sell his book through media appearances. It is estimated that after Mackay appeared on *Oprah Winfrey* (with up to 16 million viewers), well over 35,000 consumers headed for the bookstores to buy *Swim With The Sharks*. Before the dizzying media tour began, Harvey launched a double-punch sales campaign that no author before him ever had conceived.

"We developed a special mailing to 5,000 bookstore managers in advance of the inventory shipment of my book. The envelope was manufactured by our company, it had a nice little gold seal and a bright red shark. The letter outlined the sales strategy, it contained the endorsements and excerpts from the book and other selling information. I had the publisher's salespeople add a touch of class to the mailing with personalized notes. Then I made a stop at Ingram Books in Nashville, Tennessee. Ingram is the country's largest book wholesaler. After meeting with the president, I met with their telephone salespeople who are in touch with those 5,000 bookstores across the country. I gave each one a copy of my book and a golden shark pin. They found out that I was a human being and I found out that these people seldom see an author. So when any of the 5,000 bookstores call them up and order 27 Iacoccas and 40 Trumps, they may say, 'Oh, incidentally, we've got *Swim With The Sharks*... do you want to

action PLAN

1 Defy the odds. Mackay didn't let the long odds of writing and publishing a bestseller deter him. Even when you think the biggest prospects, the biggest goals are beyond your reach, don't give up. When the tide turns against you, what can you do every day to maintain a good attitude and a good effort?

2 Polish and revise your sales strategy. When he found out the first draft of *Swim With The Sharks* didn't measure up, Mackay edited and revised his work. To continuously improve your sales, continuously refine and improve your skills. How can you make small improvements to even your time-tested strategies?

3 Do the little things well. The gold seal and red shark on Mackay's envelopes are little details that make a big difference. Taking care of such small details as sending greeting cards on special occasions or handling problems personally can help you retain buyers. What details do you overlook and how can you take care of them to exceed customer expectations?

try 30 of those?' The selling lesson? Little things mean a lot. Not true. Little things mean everything!"

THE BIG PAYOFF

Harvey's book made it to the bestseller list within the first two weeks of publication. His strategy of doing his homework paid off. William Morrow knew that they had a hit on their hands and organized an auction to sell the paperback rights to Harvey's new book.

"One day the president of William Morrow called to tell me about the auction. I asked, 'How many bidders will be there?' He said, 'About six.' I said, 'I'd like to meet them before they bid.' He replied, 'You can't do that, it's never been done before.' I told him, 'You didn't read my book. I don't want those people buying from a computer printout. I want them to see me in the flesh. I want them to see commitment. I want them to hopefully see excellence and perhaps they will think twice about it.' Within a matter of days, we sold the paperback rights for $787,500 to Fawcett. This was one of the largest paperback sales of a business book. Within weeks it catapulted to number one on *The New York Times* bestseller list." While most people can think of a hundred different things they would do once they're successful, Mackay thinks of a hundred different action steps that lead to success.

"I did a hundred little things right – the title, the subtitle, the graphics, the endorsements, the rewriting, the direct mail, the personal visits, the hundreds of phone calls, the research, the media blitz, the sales strategy, all on top of the small job of writing a good book in the first place."

Mackay was so convinced that his book would make it that he even persuaded his publisher to offer a complete money-back guarantee to every consumer. Of the 600,000 hardcover copies sold, fewer than a dozen were returned.

The sales lesson: "Believe in yourself, even when nobody else does."

Benchmarking YOUR SUCCESS

To swim with the sharks and stay afloat, you need more than a life preserver. Arm yourself with innovation, testimonials and a commitment to success, and take Harvey Mackay's other suggestions to work yourself into a selling frenzy. Take this quiz to see if you have the skills to keep your head above water, and what to do if your score is less than perfect.

⑤=Always, ④=Often, ③=Sometimes, ②=Rarely, ①=Never

1. I believe in myself and my ability to succeed even where others have failed.

     ⑤   ④   ③   ②   ①

2. I regularly collect testimonials from happy customers and use them in my presentations and promotions.

     ⑤   ④   ③   ②   ①

3. I know the value of good business contacts and strive to meet new people and strengthen my current relationships.

     ⑤   ④   ③   ②   ①

4. I pay attention to detail in my actions, appearance, written work and in other areas that reflect on me.

     ⑤   ④   ③   ②   ①

5. I am willing to do the legwork — making phone and face-to-face calls, staying in the trenches — to earn new customers.

     ⑤   ④   ③   ②   ①

6. I try to differentiate my products and myself with creative thinking and innovative ideas.

     ⑤   ④   ③   ②   ①

Your Total _____

Your Final Score: Add your score for each question to get your final score. If you scored:

From 25 to 30 points: You are a strong swimmer — just don't rest on your laurels. "After a hit," says Mackay, "many people lose their intensity," but you can maintain yours the way he does — by constantly challenging yourself.

From 18 to 24 points: To achieve success, commit to it. Ask yourself if you will put in the hours, do the legwork and take care of the details — in other words, do the things that turn dreams of achievement into reality. To boost your momentum, set realistic goals and monitor your progress.

Below 18 points: Reevaluate your actions and your attitude. Build your confidence by improving your self-talk — remember that some of history's biggest successes were once failures too. Your brain is your best sales tool, so use it to think of novel ways to prospect or sell.

FOLLOWING IN HIS FATHER'S CUSTOMER-FOCUSED

FOOTSTEPS, J.W. MARRIOTT JR. HAS BUILT A

$9 BILLION HOTEL AND REAL ESTATE EMPIRE.

PHOTO BY PHILIP BERMINGHAM PHOTOGRAPHY

J.W. Marriott Jr.

With an unparalleled attention to customer needs the Marriott family built a roadside root beer stand into a lodging giant. This article will help you learn from their success and turn your organization into a customer-driven powerhouse. If corporate America ever builds a hall of fame for customer service, it should dedicate an entire wing solely to the Marriott organization. Since J. Willard Marriott Sr. opened his first curbside restaurant in 1927, the company he founded has never wavered from one unifying goal: to deliver exceptional service to every Marriott customer. With a perfectionist's attention to detail coupled with the fundamental belief that people truly make a difference, J.W. Marriott Jr. has carried on his father's legacy to create a service-driven lodging and food service empire.

fascinating fact

Marriott International offers more than 229,000 rooms worldwide.

Second-generation Marriott International CEO J. W. "Bill" Marriott Jr. says that he gained invaluable lessons in customer service from his father's fanatically detail-oriented approach to running a chain of restaurants.

"Long before he got into the hotel business my father was primarily a restaurant owner," Marriott explains. "By watching him and going around to our restaurants with him I came to understand the importance of an absolute adherence to quality. He never tolerated anything less than perfection in operations. When he went into a restaurant he examined everything, from how clean the counters were to the food's freshness. Then he would go through waitress lineups to make sure their uniforms were starched, shoes and stockings straight and that they knew the menu and the daily specials. Nothing escaped his eye. Admittedly, he was very tough, but that was because his whole philosophy in business was to take care of the customer. So everything was focused on delivering that customer value and a really terrific end product."

According to Bill Marriott, despite the senior Marriott's toughness he was still able to communicate his affection for his employees.

"When I first started out in the business, I just couldn't believe that he was never satisfied. I thought things were pretty good, and he'd always find something wrong with everything that was being done. Even when people tried extremely hard to do a good job, he had a great knack for simultaneously telling them how bad they were but also that he still loved them.

"It was the old ham sandwich routine; he'd give them a kick, a kiss and a kick. He was great at telling people that they weren't measuring up, while also telling

---

A History of Serving the Customer

From attention to the slightest detail of food preparation to serving a customer's every need, two generations of Marriotts have developed a structure of success.

achievement LESSONS

1927 J. Willard Marriott and wife Allie open nine-seat root beer stand in Washington, DC. With the later addition of hot food the stand was renamed The Hot Shoppe.

1929 Marriott officially incorporated as Hot Shoppes, Inc.

1937 Marriott pioneers in-flight catering service at Washington's old Hoover Airfield (current site of the Pentagon), serving Eastern, American and Capital Airlines.

1953 First company public stock offering at $10.25 per share. Offering sells out in two hours.

1957 Marriott opens first hotel, the Twin Bridges Marriott Motor Hotel in Arlington, VA.

1964 Company name changes to Marriott-Hot Shoppes, Inc., and J.W. Marriott Jr. elected president at age 32. 1964 annual sales: $85 million.

1972 J.W. Marriott Jr. succeeds his father as chief executive officer.

1982 Company acquires Host International, becoming the country's largest operator of airport terminal concessions.

1983 First moderately priced "Courtyard by Marriott" hotels open near Atlanta, GA.

1985 J.W. Marriott Sr. passes away at New Hampshire summer home at the age of 84. J.W. Marriott Jr. named chairman of the board.

1989 Marriott announces corporate restructuring. Plan includes sale of company's fast food and family restaurants. 1989 company revenues: $7.5 billion.

1993 Marriott Corporation splits: Marriott International to manage lodging and service businesses; Host Marriott Corp. to focus on real estate and airport and toll-road concessions.

them that he knew they could measure up and that he expected them to do better. He had a great affinity for his people and they had a great affinity for him."

Besides an eye for details, Bill Marriott emphasizes the impact his father's perseverance made on the future CEO.

"The other important lesson I learned from my father was 'Never give up,'" Marriott says. "He was always determined to stay with something until he achieved it, no matter what the odds. He started out with absolutely nothing, and eventually built a really terrific company. A lot of that success stemmed from his unwillingness to give up or to accept anything short of the very best.

"The story I like to tell about my father that really sums it all up is about the day he died. It was at a family cookout in New Hampshire. We had corn on the cob, and there were two pieces left, one fresh and one stale piece. We argued about who was going to get the fresh piece. He wanted me to have it and I wanted him to have it, and finally I got him to take it. After we both ate our corn, he got up from the table and said, 'We've got to get some better corn around here.' Then he went into the living room, sat down and died. To the very end he kept insisting on getting the best. That's what I remember most about him."

> ## fascinating fact
>
> *Last year,* Fortune *named Marriott one of the 100 best companies to work for in America.*

A NEW DIRECTION FOR GROWTH

By the time Bill Marriott became president of the Marriott Corporation in 1964, the company had grown to encompass 45 Hot Shoppes restaurants, four hotels and a fledgling airline catering company. The new president soon realized that in the restaurant business, it is almost impossible to maintain both rapid growth and control over quality standards.

"In the 1960s we got into fast food," Marriott explains. "But in the fast food industry you can't grow by owning and running every restaurant. But my father was dead set against franchising because he had seen his friend Howard Johnson franchise and then lose control of his business.

"I realized that in the hotel business we could make more money in two or three hotels than in a hundred restaurants, and it's not as difficult a management job. Trying to run 100 restaurants is murder. When I became president I would go to 12 restaurants and six of them would be great while the other six would be terrible. Then I'd go back a week later and the situation would be reversed; the six terrible ones would be great but the six great ones would be terrible. There was never any consistency and it was driving me nuts. So I decided that since the hotel business was both more profitable and simpler to manage, that was the best direction for the company."

While the elder Marriott left a perfectionist legacy on company kitchens and dining rooms, since assuming the company's reins Bill Marriott has made the hotel side of the business uniquely his. In addition to the detail-oriented lessons and never-say-die attitude learned under his father's wing, Marriott has created a service organization driven exclusively by the needs of the customer.

In addition Marriott has exploited the changing needs of American business with canny insight. As suburban business centers arose in the 1960s and 1970s, Marriott built hotels offering ready access to airports, office complexes and heavily traveled beltways and freeways. And by offering group rates, banquet facilities and other amenities, Marriott provided a genuine competitive advantage over competitors to mid-to-upper-range business travelers.

RESEARCH MOVES MARRIOTT FORWARD

By the early 1980s Marriott realized that the traditional full-service hotel market had reached its upper potential. To maintain growth, Marriott looked to its Procter & Gamble-inspired market research apparatus. That research showed customers who were generally satisfied with hotels in the upper and lower ends of the market. Such mid-price hotel chains as Holiday Inn and Quality Inn were vulnerable to a competitor that could offer consistent service for a moderate price.

Enter "Courtyard by Marriott." Without bellhops, room service and many of the other extras that helped make previous Marriott hotels successful, the new entry into the hotel market debuted in 1983 providing travelers with consistently high-quality rooms at a budget-conscious price. The Courtyards' cookie-cutter design permitted rapid construction and, by 1989, more than 100 of these highly successful hotels were operating throughout the country.

Market research also helps Marriott cater to customers' needs in specific locales. To attract members of the local community, Marriott hotel and resort restaurants offer menus featuring regional cuisine as well as wallet-friendly value meals and "early bird" specials. Pizza prepared on the premises and solo dining areas featuring accelerated service are among the other specialized amenities Marriott restaurants offer. Market research suggesting that seafood could draw both locals as well as hotel guests led directly to the moderately priced Sea Grill restaurants, now featured in more than 15 Marriotts nationwide.

Although extensive market research often tips the competition to plans in the works before actually getting a product or service going, Marriott rises to the challenge by being better, faster and more economical. In April 1993, for example, Marriott introduced the Marriott Miles program. Members can earn frequent-flyer miles with six different airlines simply by staying at Marriott, regardless of whether they flew on that airline, or at all for that matter. As Joe Brancatelli of *Frequent Flyer* magazine says, "Marriott Miles may not offer anything newer than Hilton's or Hyatt's guest programs, but Marriott just packaged it better."

> ### fascinating fact
>
> *Marriott International reported a net income of $335 million in 1997.*

Today Marriott continues its never-ending quest to find the most effective ways to deliver what Bill Marriott calls "a really terrific end product." "We have an awful lot of ways to determine exactly what a Marriott customer values," he explains. "One way is through focus groups that actively seek out customers and talk to them. To make these focus groups as diverse as possible, we target input from all Marriott customers, including business transients, men and women who travel just on business, associations – as many different important demographics as we can reach.

"We also recently did a tracking study where we interviewed 700 different customers for 30 minutes each about their lodging experiences. We asked them everything from what they thought specifically about Marriott in terms of our strengths versus what needs improving, to what their experiences had been with other chains. We like to do this kind of customer research regularly because we want to know exactly where we stand with the customer. The more you know about the customer the better job you can do."

THE FIVE KEY DRIVERS

Extensive market research is hardly unique to Marriott. But while other companies may survey their customers to the brink of exhaustion with little genuine change resulting, Marriott implements customer-driven changes faster than any competitor. As an example, Bill Marriott describes the process Marriott went through after determining the most important elements driving a positive hotel guest experience.

"After extensive research," he explains, "we found that customers at full-service Marriotts all want five things: a great breakfast, fast check-in, fast check-out, clean rooms and friendly service. And they want those five things consistently. And so we took them one by one. We said, 'All right, number one, what's the problem with breakfast?' The main problem was that waitresses were not in the dining room because they're running back to the kitchen to get toast or to wait for an order, and meanwhile a customer is looking around for his waitress so he can get out quickly. So we're now putting runners in the kitchen to bring out your food from the kitchen to the dining room. And in addition to putting more people in the kitchens to assemble orders we've actually moved a lot of the cooking into the dining room itself.

"Number two, to speed the check-in process we've installed what we call the 'First 10 program,' where we bypass the front desk by preregistering guests, meeting them at the door and immediately giving them the key to their rooms. Number three, for fast check-out we now slide the bill under the door at 4 a.m. so all guests have to do is pick up the bill, sign it and they're checked out. I spoke to a customer the other day who said that he stood in line for 40 minutes waiting to check out of a competitor's hotel. He was furious, and he was a big customer of theirs."

The fourth key customer issue was clean rooms. To make sure rooms are in full working condition before a customer crosses the threshold Marriott has implemented a room-by-room monitoring system. Maids must follow a 54-step process in preparing rooms to make sure they are clean and that all electrical appliances, from TVs to air conditioners, are fully functional.

"The system is better now," Marriott says, "because it's easier to eliminate problems. If we have a toilet overflowing in one room more than once, we know that the toilet in that room has a problem. Before, we would have kept fixing it without keeping any record, but now we can see by the tracking system that room 401 has had a toilet problem twice in a row and we can replace the toilet."

GOING THE EXTRA MILE

As for number five, friendly service, Marriott has long been renowned for competent, amiable and efficient employees. "Chairman Bill," as many Marriott employees refer to the CEO, believes that his people deliver superior service because they have an emotional investment in making customers happy. To emphasize this belief he refers to all individuals on the Marriott payroll as "associates."

"Our basic philosophy," he explains, "is to make sure our associates are very happy and that they work to go the extra mile – take care of customers and have fun doing it. A lot of companies go through the motions but they don't go the extra mile."

The first step in going that extra mile means making the effort to hire the right people. Well aware that in today's business environment no company can expect to

action
PLAN

1 Sweat the small stuff. From clean counters to straight stockings, J.W. Marriott Sr. knew little things mean a lot. What areas of quality or service have you neglected and how can you bring them up to par?

2 Insist on the best. Bill Marriott says his father "was never satisfied" with the quality of his restaurants – an attitude that helps ensure ongoing improvement. How can you continually raise your standards of quality and service to keep your customers happy?

3 Gather feedback. At Marriott, the customer's opinion counts, and the company has "an awful lot of ways to determine exactly what a Marriott customer values," says Chairman Bill. What will you do to show customers their feedback is important and to collect more of it?

4 Make changes. The VIPs at Marriott found out what customers wanted, then used it to improve their product. Once you learn what your buyers want, how much and how quickly will you change to meet their needs?

sit back and attract the best people through good karma alone, Marriott has developed a marketing approach to sell the company to prospective "associates." As Senior Vice President Clifford Ehrlich says, "We approach it by saying we have jobs we're trying to sell, and the prospective work force out there are the buyers." In addition, Marriott focuses significant effort on retaining and promoting from within employees that have proven themselves capable.

As a result, more than a third of the company's managers have moved up from hourly wage positions. Once they're on board, Marriott attempts to give associates the greatest possible amount of freedom and autonomy that corporate policies will allow. Another term for the extra mile at Marriott is "discretionary effort."

"That discretionary effort is usually the difference between a good hospitality experience and a bad one," Ehrlich explains. "In the service business, tapping into the discretionary effort that people come to work with is very important. The trick in management is creating an environment in which people can contribute to the success of the business. You can't practice a lot of strict top-down management and achieve that."

Marriott accomplishes the elusive goal of employee empowerment by allowing associates to determine for themselves how their days will be spent and using the "one uniform concept," which eliminates strict job classifications among associates. At Marriott hotels, for example, every employee is cross-trained to handle all major guest services.

PRESSING THE FLESH

Chairman Bill genuinely cares about what Marriott's associates have to say about the way the company is being run. He logs an average of 200,000 travel miles every year visiting Marriotts, inspecting and talking to associates.

"I used to be able to visit every hotel every year," Marriott says, "but these days I can only get to between 150 and 200. When I get to the hotels, I usually go first to the front desk to let those people know that I understand how important they are in helping customers begin their experience with us in a positive way.

"Then I head for the kitchen to see if it's clean, if the food's fresh, if they have the right uniforms on, etc. I also like to see how the associates react. Are they happy to see me? Do they want to have their pictures taken with me? What is their level of enthusiasm? How do they like their boss? At one hotel the boss and I went into the laundry. The laundry people said to him, 'Hey boss, why didn't you come see us yesterday? You've been down in the laundry every day and you missed yesterday. Where were you?' And to me that's a great sign that he's a good manager. He's out of the office, with his people, and they appreciate and love him for it.

"When managers are out with their people and with customers instead of sitting in their offices, productivity is higher and guest satisfaction is higher. But basically, when I meet with the associates, I just want to do whatever I can to let them know that they're important to me."

Although some employees might have mixed emotions about these spot inspections from the CEO, they nonetheless appreciate the opportunity to speak directly with the man at the top. He places a tremendous value on these encounters as well.

"CEOs don't listen enough," Marriott says. "The people who work for them know more about their particular areas than the chief executive does. It's only from the associates on the front lines that I can perhaps learn about unique practices that I can then take and apply to other hotels." But even the globe-trotting CEO cannot meet with each of Marriott's employees. For this reason company policy states that any Marriott employee with a grievance who has not seen action after meeting with a supervisor can go directly to the chairman. Although this rarely occurs, Marriott claims that in more than one case he has interceded on an associate's behalf.

"One woman approached me," he explains, "and said she was a cocktail waitress at the Marriott Marquis in New York. She complained that the shoes they were required to wear were too high and caused pain in their backs and legs. I told the people there, 'Get them some lower pumps, guys.' If they're not comfortable, and if their backs ache, then they're going to growl at our customers."

The results for the customer tend to be anything but ordinary, as in the case of the U.S. invasion of Panama when Marriott employees risked their lives to hide American guests in the laundry room dryers. Common courtesy can produce genuinely uncommon valor. At Marriott, fanatical customer service, perfectionism and attention to detail are learned, not inherited habits. ▣

Benchmarking
YOUR SUCCESS

Marriott achieved success by keeping the focus where it belongs — on the customer. As Zig Ziglar says, "If you help enough other people get what they want, you'll get what you want." Take this quiz to see if your service strategy measures up to Marriott's, then start your improvement efforts with the suggestions provided afterward.

⑤=Always, ④=Often, ③=Sometimes, ②=Rarely, ①=Never

1. When customers tell me what they like or dislike about my performance, I change to please them.

⑤ ④ ③ ② ①

2. I keep all my promises and try to deliver something extra.

⑤ ④ ③ ② ①

3. I often ask customers to rate my performance and tell me how I can improve.

⑤ ④ ③ ② ①

4. I see my buyers as individuals and try to tailor my proposals specifically to their needs.

⑤ ④ ③ ② ①

5. I thank my customers often for their business, and send cards and/or other small surprises to make them feel appreciated.

⑤ ④ ③ ② ①

6. I treat every aspect of my product and service as though it were of critical importance to the customer.

⑤ ④ ③ ② ①

Your Total _____

Your Final Score: Add your score for each question to get your final score. If you scored:

From 25 to 30 points: You treat your customers like gold. Continue to make them feel special even when they haven't bought recently, and keep track of your competitors' products and services to make sure you still have an advantage.

From 18 to 24 points: If you value your buyers, they probably don't know it. Getting close to them should increase your desire to serve them well, so stay in touch with them and don't limit conversations to business. To keep you on your toes, send out "report cards" they can use to rate your performance.

Below 18 points: Take your customers for granted, and they'll take their business elsewhere. Remember that they are the source of your sales, and rework your selling strategy to include gestures of gratitude and techniques for learning more about them. Approach and maintain every relationship with the future in mind.

1921 - 1989

YOUR SUCCESS WAS HIS BUSINESS.

NOW TURN EARL NIGHTINGALE'S STRANGEST

SECRETS OF MIND MANAGEMENT, INTEGRITY,

EDUCATION AND OTHER SUCCESS FACTORS

INTO YOUR GREATEST DISCOVERY.

Earl Nightingale

Earl Nightingale, the co-founder of Nightingale-Conant Corporation, has been at the forefront of the motivation and success field for almost 40 years. He has read everything from Zane Grey and Napoleon Hill to George Santayana and Ralph Waldo Emerson. His early life was propelled by the books he read, while his young adulthood centered around his personal search for the psychological and intellectual secrets of success. During his 66 years he has seen disappointment (his father walked out one day leaving Earl's mother with three young sons when Earl was no more than 11); tragedy (Earl joined the Marine Corps and was nearly blown to bits at his station on the top of the main mast on the battleship *Arizona* when it was bombed by the Japanese during their surprise attack on Pearl Harbor); and hardship (his first years in radio trying to find sponsors for his motivational show were a difficult uphill climb).

In an exclusive interview *Selling Power* conducted two years before his death, Earl Nightingale, radio star, author, entrepreneur/businessman and motivator to a nation discussed his views on success and disappointment, and told *Selling Power* readers what miracles the mind can work, if only we can unlock its untold powers. Earl's latest book, *Earl Nightingale's Greatest Discovery,* has just been released by Dodd, Mead & Company Inc., New York.

Though he is the first to acknowledge the huge contribution books have made to his education, attitude and success, he maintains that no specific vol-

> ## fascinating fact
>
> *When Earl Nightingale won Toastmaster International's Golden Gavel Award in 1976, his radio show,* Our Changing World, *was the world's most widely heard program.*

Earl Nightingale's love of learning kept him at the head of the class for life. In such books as Napoleon Hill's *Think and Grow Rich* he found the secrets of success and inspiration to try them himself. To take your success to new heights, remember that knowledge is power. With these measures you can engage your brain and make information your ally.

Learn to think. Nightingale notes that in school we learn to memorize, but in life we must be able to think. To learn how, he says we must see our minds as companions and leaders on the path we choose to follow. Think about where you want your life to lead, then write your thoughts down in the form of a plan. When you do, Nightingale says, "it seems that all the forces in the world begin to come to your aid."

achievement LESSONS

Read. In his library of works by great thinkers, Nightingale finds both education and motivation. "You can't read these people without getting a little excited by everything in the world," he says. The right books can do the same for you. Carefully select the books to start your own self-improvement library, and turn to them to inspire and inform you.

Extend your education. From birth to death we are works in progress, and Nightingale says "a person with an ongoing education has been touched and dabbed by so many great authors and great lines, great poetry, the great philosophies of the world." To be sure you end up a masterpiece, make a continuous effort to learn all that books, tapes, courses and other people have to teach.

umes stand out as the keys to his extraordinary achievements.

"You know education is a like a fine painting which has thousands of little dabs of paint, none of which you are particularly aware of but which in total comprise the finished work," explains Nightingale. "A person with an ongoing education has been touched and dabbed by so many great authors and great lines, great poetry, the great philosophies of the world."

Nightingale says he first felt the hunger for knowledge at an early age. Thanks to his innate curiosity, he got a head start on the education that would play such an important role in his life. In his search for the secrets of success, Nightingale helped to ensure his own.

"I knew when I was 12 years old that I wanted to become a writer," he says, "and that I wanted to find the secret of success which spelled the difference between men and women who are successful in life and those who are not. I was looking for the answer to that question from the time I first began reading about the great religions and philosophies of the world."

The lessons Nightingale learned helped him to sell advertising for his radio program. His lack of experience, however, proved to be a difficult obstacle that put even his endurance and persistence to the test. As Nightingale learned, a proven record of service builds trust, and that was one advantage he lacked.

"I started calling on the agencies in Chicago and telling them about my program and the fact that I could sell their products for them," says Nightingale. "I was very sincere and I was very eager but I was very young and inexperienced and of course, since I didn't have a track record, no one would try my program."

No one enjoys rejection, but Nightingale knew that letting it get to him would mean giving up his dream. Instead of letting disappointment bring him down, he maintained a steady stream of positive self-talk that eventually became a flood of success.

"I had one great thing working for me: I just wouldn't give up," he says. "I kept telling myself to stay with it. I would say to myself, 'You can make this, what you are doing is right. You have a good program, you can sell products on that show, you have a good audience and you are 100 percent dedicated to it and it will come, just stay with it.' I used to keep telling myself that even though the pickings were very slim at that time, I would ultimately succeed."

> ## fascinating fact
>
> *Nightingale's talk record,* The Strangest Secret, *won a Gold Record award for sales exceeding one million copies.*

NIGHTINGALE TAKES FLIGHT

Luck is said to be the result of preparation meeting opportunity. With a chance to audition for a children's adventure program, Nightingale answered opportunity's knock and got the break he needed to keep his hopes and his radio program afloat. Reading Napoleon Hill's *Think and Grow Rich* made this time an even greater turning point in Nightingale's life.

"There was an audition for *Sky King*, which was an adventure program for children," he says. "I won the star part and that helped me survive while I was building my own radio program. At the same time, when I was 29, I was reading *Think and Grow Rich* by Napoleon Hill. I came across six words that made a big difference in my life, 'We Become What We Think About.' When I saw that, I sat up. All of a sudden, all the lights went on and I said, 'That's it. That is what I have been reading over and over again.' That is what Buddha meant when he said, 'As the wheel follows the ox behind, we will become what our thoughts have made of us.' I realized that every great philosopher had said much the same thing in different words. I had read 'As ye believe, so shall it be done unto you.' In so many different ways I had been reading that great line over and over again. It just revolutionized my life and from that time on I have had very few problems."

After learning that we become what we think about, Nightingale knew that to control his destiny, he had to control his mind. Mind management, he says, starts with learning to think – a skill that school seldom teaches, but should.

fascinating fact

When Nightingale died in 1989, his library included 6,000 books.

"The first thing we have to do is to learn how to think. We are not taught how to think in school and most people do not think very much, if at all. We are taught in school to remember things and yet the highest function a human being is capable of is to think. That is the highest function, that is the only thing we can do that creatures in the field can't do."

Fortunately, Nightingale says we can learn. We start by trusting our minds to give us direction, then making up our minds as to what that direction should be. From your serious thought and written ideas about what you want out of life emerges the path that should lead you to it.

"We learn to think gradually ... first comes the realization that my mind is my companion, my mind is what is going to lead me to where I want to go. Then I sit down with a notepad, in my case, and a pen and I say, 'Now where do I want to go?' I have been given a miraculous holiday here on earth. Now what do I want to do with it, where do I want to go, what do I want to do?' And you begin making notes – this doesn't all come to you in a great flash of revelation. You begin thinking about it. 'Well, I think I'd like this, I think I'd like to do that, I know I would be happiest doing this particular thing.' And you begin making notes and you begin making a plan and you begin following this plan. As soon as you do, it seems that all the forces in the world begin to come to your aid."

To apply his strategy to selling, Nightingale says he views the profession from a service standpoint. Rather than focus on what he must do to sell, he concentrates on what he can do to serve.

"I approach sales from a slightly different standpoint and that is one of service. Not 'How can I sell him my product?' but 'How can I best serve this person?'"

INFUSED WITH ENTHUSIASM

Despite the sales success that attitude has brought him, Nightingale retains a healthy respect for the profession's challenges, and argues that no work of value is ever easy. If you believe strongly in your product, however, Nightingale says your enthusiasm can help see you through the difficult times.

"I don't think that any work that is important to a person is easy. It's not easy to write a book or a daily radio program. It is not easy to raise chickens if you do it well. Nothing worthwhile is easy but we develop a facility and if our basic fundamentals are right, we are going to be right. Selling has often been confused with intimidation or putting something over on somebody and of course it shouldn't be looked at that way. Of course, we are all salesmen, you know, one way or another. I'm selling ideas all the time, I'm selling education and I get very enthusiastic about that. I think you will be a very good salesman for whatever you find of great interest and you can get enthusiastic about."

To help infuse his own people with enthusiasm, Nightingale says he "studied the books at that time. Since

action PLAN

1 Manage your mind. When distractions tempt you or disappointments demotivate you, good mind management can keep you focused on your job. Earl Nightingale says the first step to mind management is learning to think. How can you learn to think more clearly, concentrate more effectively and maintain a winning attitude?

2 Work your plan. As you write down your ideas on what direction you want your life to take, Nightingale says you must shape those ideas into plan. Assess how well you plan your years, months and days. What can you do to enhance your planning skills and stay motivated to follow through on the plans you make?

3 Serve to sell. Earl Nightingale approached prospects thinking not how he could sell them, but how he could serve them. Give your buyers a reason to talk and meet with you so that they benefit even if they don't buy. How can you add more value before and after the sale to show prospects you give them more for their time and money?

I owned an insurance agency, I read all the books on selling. So I talked about what I had read in those books." Along with enthusiasm, Nightingale says several other qualities help build long-lasting and profitable selling careers – qualities salespeople and everyone else should try to develop.

"These are the same qualities that I would want anyone to develop in his life: Integrity is the first, and that means being absolutely true. Being truthful under all circumstances. Tell the truth and build a reputation for integrity. Another one would be punctuality. Another one would be to be always well dressed and neat. Still another would be to be deferential to the person to whom you are speaking, realizing that he has granted you an interview. Be respectful."

As for self-motivation, Nightingale says he understands that not everyone feels like moving full steam ahead all the time. Sometimes energy and positive thought seem to flow naturally, and sometimes they don't seem to flow at all. When Nightingale feels his motivation waning, he says he gets by with a little help from his wife, Diana, and from the friends in his library.

"Human beings are subject to moods. Sometimes they don't feel very good, sometimes they feel a little down. I feel down from time to time and I have to reach up and pull a book off the shelf and get myself charged up again. Fortunately, I have two great sources of motivation. One is my wife, Diana, who is just marvelous at that kind of thing. I just can't really stay down very long living around her. The other, of course, is my fabulous library. I have so many great thinkers, and you can't read these people without getting a little excited about everything in the world."

SUFFERING YIELDS SUCCESS

Even with a great library of motivational resources and the support of their loved ones, salespeople are still subject to the fear of rejection. That fear can be crippling to salespeople, but Nightingale says it doesn't have to be. The more you believe in yourself and your product, the more power you are likely to have over rejection and its effect on you.

"When I was selling life insurance, I experienced the fear of rejection, initially, going in. But I quickly got over that. When I go on an interview with a talk show host, let's say, I never know what attitude he or she is going to take. He might take an adversarial attitude or something. Because I really believe in what I am talking about and I am completely dedicated to it, I think I can hold my own with anybody in that field."

Nightingale could also hold his own with anyone in a contest to overcome adversity and triumph over huge disappointments. His own trials and tribulations have taught him that we all have to take the good with the bad, that life isn't fair but that often suffering is a precursor to huge rewards. When disappointment strikes, the grace with which we handle it determines how well we will recover.

"It's difficult to handle disappointment, but I think that a well-adjusted person realizes that it is part of living and takes a big deep breath and starts out again. Maybe rests a little bit before going at it again. I have had a lot of disappointments, but you know they have usually led on to other successes, to additional successes. I know that there have been times when I thought, 'I'm terribly sorry that this is happening but I realize that maybe I'm being led to another slightly different direction in order to achieve these things that I want to achieve.' There is no success without suffering. There is an old legend that goes, 'If you succeed without suffering, it is because someone has suffered for you. If you suffer without succeeding, it is so someone may succeed after you, but there is no success without suffering.' I think that the word 'suffering' was meant to mean 'tremendous amount of effort and dedication.' Success is an effect and you have got to have a cause and that is the work or whatever you do to achieve that success."

> ## fascinating fact
>
> *Nightingale was one of only 12 Marines to survive the Pearl Harbor attack on the U.S.S. Arizona.*

None of us is immune to misfortune, and as much as we may want to know the reasons why bad things happen to good people, searching for answers that simply aren't there can add to our frustration. No stranger to pain and hardship, Nightingale prefers to keep the reasons behind it mystery, and finds beauty and comfort in accepting what happens to him and making the best of it instead of analyzing it.

"My early years were pretty tough, as were the war years. I have done my share of suffering. I have had a number of physical problems that have had to be overcome. I had a heart valve replaced, but long before that I had two brain tumors removed and I have had both shoulders and hips replaced because of arthritis. I am familiar with pain. We are like old friends. However, I look at it this way. We have been granted a short time and we don't understand that life is a mystery. It doesn't bother me, mysteries don't bother me. Some people can't stand mysteries, they want answers for everything. I can live with a mystery. We came from a mystery and we are going to go into a mystery and I think that is beautiful and wonderful. We know there is something there and I tend to believe that it is going to be great. I want to do the best I can with this life and then if there is another one, I will do the best I can with that one."

Few would disagree that Earl Nightingale has made the most of his time here. He is successful by any standard and on many different levels. His own measure of success is that we be in the driver's seats of our lives, and his advice to help others do that is simple.

"Success doesn't come in a big flash. It comes from a result of steady daily work over a long period of time. First, find the right work. Second, do the things you most enjoy doing. Third, set exciting and worthwhile goals that will mean a great deal to you when you achieve them, whatever they happen to be." ▣

To co-found Nightingale-Conant and rise to fame as a radio celebrity, author and motivator, Earl Nightingale practiced persistence, mind management and service. To sell by the same rules, take this quiz and check your score.

⑤=Always, ④=Often, ③=Sometimes, ②=Rarely, ①=Never

1. I maintain high standards of integrity for myself and am completely truthful with my buyers.

   ⑤　　④　　③　　②　　①

2. I take responsibility for motivating myself and I give myself an attitude adjustment when I need it.

   ⑤　　④　　③　　②　　①

3. I understand the value of ideas and education and take steps to learn all I need to know to achieve my goals

   ⑤　　④　　③　　②　　①

4. When I know my buyer needs my product, I don't let a rejection keep me from making a sale.

   ⑤　　④　　③　　②　　①

5. I know that serving buyers helps me sell more, and I make sure I can help them before I try to sell to them.

   ⑤　　④　　③　　②　　①

6. I recognize that sacrifice is key to success and am willing to work hard to increase my income and grow professionally

   ⑤　　④　　③　　②　　①

Your Total _____

Your Final Score Add your score for each question to get your final score. If you scored:

From 25 to 30 points: You have Earl Nightingale's winning mindset, and your curiosity and willingness to learn give you the tools to reach your potential. To sell your way to the top, remember to implement what you learn, refine it and retain it for future use.

From 18 to 24 points: Professional sales has its lows as well as its highs. Prepare yourself to face obstacles and setbacks by training your brain. Revise your attitude toward temporary failures and educate yourself in a variety of ways (books, tapes, fellow salespeople) to prevent more of them. Keep in mind that you have to control your thoughts in order to control your life.

Below 18 points: You hold the key to your own freedom but you must take the initiative to learn to use it. Take a lesson from a master motivator to get your attitude in order, and make a list of resources you can consult daily to improve critical selling skills. After two or three months, compare your current performance with your past achievements to see how much you've improved.

HE INVENTED THE SALES MANUAL, THE

PRESENTATION, THE TERRITORY, THE QUOTA,

SALES TRAINING AND MORE. HIS IDEAS

ARE STILL AT WORK TODAY.

John Henry
Patterson

The greatest salesman of all time was born nearly a century and a half ago on a farm in Ohio. His name was John Henry Patterson, and if he were alive today he'd fire most of the salespeople reading this chapter. Brilliant, innovative, dictatorial and mercurial, Patterson is best remembered today as the founder of the National Cash Register Company.

More significantly, but virtually forgotten, this mustachioed, bespectacled whirlwind of a man invented modern selling. The sales training manual, canned presentation, protected territory and quota system were all products of Patterson's fertile mind. So were sales meetings, direct mail, testimonials, industrial advertising and publicity.

So numerous were his contributions and vast was his influence that Patterson may rightly be called the father of professional selling. And perhaps even the father of the modern American corporation, for many of those whom Patterson trained went on to found corporations such as IBM and Burroughs.

Single-handedly, and often opposed by business associates and the very salesmen who benefited from his genius, Patterson created the greatest selling machine this country has ever seen. It may even be said that no company today approaches the marketplace efficiency that Patterson's NCR achieved in its hey-

> ## fascinating fact
>
> *After NCR opened a dining room for 400 women in 1895, the sick list dropped from 18 percent to 2 percent in one week.*

Patterson's Sales Innovations

1884: Exclusive territories Patterson purchased The National Cash Register Company and began to hire sales agents across the nation. To create extra incentive, Patterson gave each agent an exclusive territory.

1885: Customer testimonials Patterson asked his sales force to collect testimonial letters. These letters became the basis of sales brochures that NCR produced for each major industry segment.

achievement
LESSONS

1887: Sales conventions Nine NCR sales agents attended the first sales convention in Dayton, Ohio. The following year Patterson wrote to his agents, "We can assure you that all who will attend, that they will be fitted to sell twice as many registers..." The result: 41 sales agents participated in the three-day event.

1888: Direct marketing Patterson believed that "Sales make news, and the news of sales makes for more sales." He asked NCR agents to collect business cards from their prospects in order to develop a mailing list. In 1888 NCR mailed 135,000 copies of a sales letter that touted the benefits of using an NCR cash register. By 1913, NCR was mailing more than nine million promotional pieces.

1890: Woman managers Well-educated working women could expect to advance quickly to supervisory jobs within NCR. Amy Acton, who became NCR's counselor-at-law, is believed to be the first woman lawyer hired by a corporation.

1892: Sales presentation Patterson charged his brother-in-law, Joseph H. Crane, with creating a standardized sales presentation. NCR salespeople were required to memorize the 450-word presentation (and were fired if they refused).

1893: Sales training Visiting his company's booth at the 1893 World's Fair, Patterson found that NCR salespeople did not how to sell the cash registers being exhibited. He immediately sequestered the salespeople in a hotel room for a quick training class. This impromptu session was so successful that Patterson instituted regular sales training for all NCR salespeople. Patterson later wrote: "It is said that salesmen are born, not made. I say, salesmen are as you make them."

1894: Motivational messages Every time Patterson started a meeting, he wrote the word "Think!" on a flip chart. Soon posters with the message "Think" began to appear in NCR offices and on the factory floor. Other motivational messages reminded employees to tell the truth, avoid injuries and offer suggestions that would improve business.

1900: Sales quota system Instead of comparing the number of registers sold in each territory, Patterson introduced the revolutionary idea of market penetration. He wrote: "Experience shows that a register can be sold for every 400 people in every town in the U.S." Armed with the latest demographic data on each territory, Patterson developed a fair and equitable sales quota system.

day. Too frequently the practices he pioneered are preached but not followed.

Rest assured that wouldn't be the case if Patterson still walked the earth. Many a head – even illustrious ones – would roll. But sales productivity would soar to peaks not seen in this country since the turn of the century.

Few companies have had more inauspicious beginnings than NCR. When Patterson, at the age of 40, bought controlling interest in the failing Dayton, Ohio, firm in 1884, there was really no market demand for cash registers. Fewer than 400 had ever been sold. There were several reasons for this. Few retail businesses, the targeted market, appreciated the value of a device they viewed as a kind of Rube Goldberg machine. Clerks, who felt the cash register represented a mechanical intruder sent to spy on their integrity, were openly hostile to salesmen who came through the door lugging a demonstration cash register. Poor craftsmanship sometimes forced the return of thousands of dollars worth of machines.

> ## fascinating fact
>
> *The first NCR factory building was built on the Patterson farm in 1888.*

Finally, there was the problem of the salesmen themselves. Slovenly, disorganized, ill-prepared and uncommitted to either the company or product, they almost seemed to stand in the way of sales.

These problems would have sunk most entrepreneurs with a fledgling business, but not Patterson. He was one of those rare human beings whose vision and resoluteness enabled him to divine solutions where others saw only a quagmire of frustration.

An anecdote from Patterson's life illustrates these qualities. Years after NCR was well-established, Patterson was told by legal advisors that his plans to incorporate NCR in Ohio would be thwarted by state law unless he reduced the number of people on NCR's board. The wiry Patterson thundered: "Don't change directors. Change the law." They did.

It was with the same single-mindedness that Patterson set out to transform NCR. A salesman first and foremost, he believed that improving salesmanship was the surest path to success, and that was where he concentrated his efforts. Just as he could command his attorneys to change a state law, so Patterson set out to change the art of selling.

CREATING A DEMAND

Patterson was one of the first in the country sold – through personal experience – on the value of the cash register. A pair of registers he bought for his retail store cut his debt from $16,000 to $3,000 in six months and helped him show a profit of $5,000. It was that experience that led him to buy the company.

But Patterson was virtually alone as a true believer. So when he bought the company that would become NCR, his first task was to create awareness of and then demand for the product.

Patterson did this in a way that stunned the business community of the day: through the heavy (even relentless) use of advertising, direct mail and publicity. In so doing, he raised advertising and promotion to unprecedented levels of sophistication, and created models still in use today.

Often it was a process of trial and error. In his first direct mail effort, Patterson spent thousands of dollars developing a circular for 5,000 prospects. "It was a good piece, but it did not contain a picture of the cash register," said Patterson. Not one response came in to NCR.

Still convinced of the value of direct mail, Patterson continued his experiments, learning as he went and distributing circulars by the millions. Some were in letter form, some carried pictures, others dramatized the use of the cash register. Many were in the form of publications directed to specific groups of retailers. To thwart antagonistic retail clerks, Patterson devised the idea of using plain envelopes, and often had the pieces mailed from cities other than Dayton.

In an inspired moment, Patterson hit on the idea of incorporating praise from satisfied customers in direct mail. These testimonials proved among the strongest cases ever devised to sway prospects. They were living arguments to buy.

Patterson spent a fortune on paving the way for his sales force through the mail. Stockholders and employees tore their hair out at the expense, and the post office had to hire additional postal clerks just to handle the influx from NCR mailings.

Not content to rely on direct mail, Patterson turned his attention to print advertising. At the time, advertising was most notable for its stuffiness, reliance on baroque graphics and lengthy, tedious copy. Patterson did for advertising what

Frank Lloyd Wright did for architecture – simplified it and made it easier on the eye. Not incidentally, he vastly improved its effectiveness.

Patterson's motto for NCR ad copywriters was "be direct and simple." Copy was kept brief and to the point. Ads were printed in plain type styles and were broken up with ample blank space. Patterson liked pictures galore in his ads, provided they were pleasant, upbeat and "something out of the ordinary" to attract attention.

In conjunction with direct mail and print advertising, Patterson also developed the industrial publicity release. "Business is news," he believed, and so hired publicists to generate articles by the score on NCR products and activities.

In the end, Patterson's "wild ideas" about promotion were upheld. Prospects who had never before heard of the cash register, let alone NCR, were regularly bombarded with a cleverly coordinated mixture of direct mail flyers, print ads and NCR articles. Those who had previously been unaware of the product suddenly began to develop a need for it.

Unfortunately, the sales force wasn't always in shape to take advantage of Patterson's ingenious efforts. Many knew less about NCR products than did the copywriters!

> ## fascinating fact
>
> *NCR's millionth machine was manufactured in its Dayton, Ohio, plant in 1911.*

THE FIRST MODERN SALES FORCE

Early on, Patterson was concerned about the quality of sales, and so – in true Patterson style – he decided to learn firsthand what was happening in the field. In a period of 51 days he visited sales offices in 50 towns and cities. What he found appalled him.

"One half of our salesmen are so ignorant of their product that they will actually prevent a man from buying, even though he wanted a cash register," he said. Returning to Dayton, he proceeded to gather the sales talks of NCR's most successful salesmen, writing up every known selling point for the cash register. The document became one of the first canned sales presentations, the *NCR Primer*.

action PLAN

1 Promote your product. To sell his profit-generating cash registers, John Henry Patterson knew he had to spread the word about them. Good promotion tells prospects about your product and why they should buy. How can you get your message out to a larger audience of new prospects and keep current ones informed?

2 Invest in education. Patterson pioneered sales training, knowing salespeople must be informed to be effective. For great salespeople, school is always in session. What people can you talk to, books can you read or courses can you take to learn more about your products, customers, competitors and new sales techniques?

3 Put lessons into practice. To help salespeople use information in the *NCR Primer* and *NCR Manual*, Patterson established training schools that doubled NCR's business. Knowledge must be implemented to make a difference. How can you translate the information you absorb into practical techniques for use on your next call?

Patterson made it a requirement that all salesmen learn the 450-word document by heart. Many of the older salesmen balked. When Patterson discovered their resistance, he implemented tests – those who failed or refused to memorize the *Primer* were fired. The remainder saw their sales soar. Reason: For the first time ever, they had a consistent presentation that covered all the important features and benefits of their products.

The *Primer* was soon followed by the *Book of Arguments*, which later developed into the *NCR Manual*, a compendium of answers to every kind of question a prospect might ask. The *Manual* was the first-ever systematic approach to handling customer objections. It also discussed topics such as introductions, first interviews, critical sales situations, and closing arguments. Like the *Primer*, it was drawn from the minds of the best NCR salesmen and compiled, again, with the goal of establishing consistency.

Many salespeople today would benefit from the wisdom of the *NCR Manual*. Always it had one objective: to make the prospect understand the proposition, not merely to batter and cajole him or her into placing an order or to win in a series of arguments – still major stumbling blocks in the 1990s.

THE BIRTH OF SALES TRAINING

Providing the *Primer* and *Manual* was one thing; ensuring that salespeople would commit the techniques outlined therein to memory another. Even with these marvelous tools at their disposal, many balked at learning. It must have seemed to John Patterson that time and again he had to drag mule-headed salespeople to a trough that brimmed with milk and honey.

While attending the 1893 World's Fair in Chicago, Patterson stopped off at the NCR display booths and quizzed the young salesmen. To his astonishment, hardly any of them knew what they were talking about – despite all the sweat he'd devoted to creating the *Primer* and *Manual*.

Patterson promptly hauled the reps off to a hotel room for a training session. This class was nothing more nor less than a review of the most basic Q&A's about NCR products – material drawn straight from the *Primer* and *Manual*. Patterson was so delighted with the results of the impromptu session that he decided to inaugurate training schools for all of his salespeople.

The first sales training school was opened in Dayton the following spring. Though based on the timeworn teacher-pupil format, the classes were as exciting as Patterson himself – a man who once deliberately shattered a water pitcher on a podium to get the audience's attention.

With illustrations and demonstrations (and a good bit of Pattersonian drama tossed in), NCR sales training instructors coached salespeople on the very modern concept of thinking in terms of the prospect's needs rather than in terms of the product. These training sessions were really classes in the art of communication, of understanding prospects and making sure they understood the sales message.

This was a hot topic with Patterson. He was often quoted as saying that fully one half of all lost sales could be attributed to the salesperson's failure to communicate. The erring sales rep might fail to clarify a point, talk indistinctly, make confusing claims or in some way fail to relay his own mental picture to the prospect.

Patterson rectified the problem of poor communication by teaching salespeople to listen to prospects. They were taught how to modify set sales presentations depending on the type of customer and the type of sales resistance showed. Patterson even hired elocutionists to teach sales agents to speak like masters of the stage.

A firm believer in "teaching through the eye" – using charts, graphs, drawings or any other visual aid to get a point across to his sales force – Patterson told salespeople to use the same technique with prospects. Sales agents were schooled in how to "illustrate" a presentation on a scratch pad while they talked about cash registers. Later, outline charts were printed on the pads, which the salesman would complete as he developed his presentation.

Thus was born the use of graphics in the sales presentation, an idea used by many but still scorned by some salespeople nearly 100 years after Patterson developed it.

The salesmen turned out by the NCR training school were a well-honed lot. Estimates made at the time show that this training was directly responsible for doubling business in the first year.

THE REWARD SYSTEM

While Patterson demanded much of his salesmen, he gave much in return. Many of his creations, such as the sales convention, the protected territory and the quota system, were vehicles for rewarding salespeople as well as for increasing productivity.

Patterson was among the first to recognize the value of brain-storming sessions among salespeople. As a result, he decided to conduct regular sales conventions where agents could exchange ideas on selling. In an "every man for himself" era, this was a revolutionary concept. In time, the conventions also provided the opportunity to recognize and reward top achievers.

Patterson developed the protected sales territory in order to attract and keep the best salesmen. In the days B.P. (Before Patterson), salesmen commonly "milked" an area, and then moved on – often into a city or region occupied by other cash register salesmen. Needless to say, this chaotic habit of raiding one's colleague caused a lot of bickering, turnover and reduced productivity.

Patterson's solution of the protected sales territory is something every salesperson takes for granted today. In return for this guarantee, NCR agents had to live up to another of Patterson's creations, the sales quota, the first effort to obtain measurable results in selling. And they had to try another then unheard-of practice – returning, after a period of time, to customers who had already bought from NCR to try to sell to them again.

Returning to an old customer, a technique Patterson called "using the user," upset many salesmen, who were convinced it was impossible to sell twice to the same prospect. As usual, Patterson was right and the objectors were wrong. Not only did past customers prove a fertile field for new sales, they were also a source of testimonials for advertising and promotions.

PATTERSON'S SIGNIFICANCE TODAY

It's all fine and well to pay tribute to a man like Patterson. Certainly sales professionals and sales managers owe him a debt of gratitude. But after this laudatory display, they would do well to go back and review Patterson's contributions. Not only were his selling techniques the most sophisticated of his day, they are – in combination – more advanced than anything practiced today. Nobody is this sophisticated now.

Billions are spent on advertising, direct mail and publicity, but rarely are these tools used as effectively as the cohesive triad Patterson forged. Salespeople still balk at learning product knowledge cold, and fail to communicate with customers. Though territories are parceled out and quotas maintained, day-to-day sales performance is not monitored as closely as it was at Patterson's NCR.

It's a pity, considering the rich heritage John Henry Patterson left to the sales profession. Perhaps more than any other American in history, he is responsible for raising the consciousness, self-image and public image of salespeople. He taught that good salespeople are made, not born. Patterson transformed an often-ridiculed job into an honored profession, and gave salespeople the skills to survive in this toughest of all callings. ▫

Benchmarking YOUR SUCCESS

As the founding father of sales, John Henry Patterson used a recipe for success that remains equally effective today. With product knowledge and promotion, objection-handling ability and Patterson's other success ingredients, you can achieve your own modern-day success. Find out if you have the right stuff — and how to get it — by taking this quiz and the advice you find next to your score.

⑤=**Always,** ④=**Often,** ③=**Sometimes,** ②=**Rarely,** ①=**Never**

1. I use newsletters, direct mail pieces, broadcast faxes and/or other methods to promote my product.

   ⑤　　　④　　　③　　　②　　　①

2. I read and learn my company and product literature and improve my sales techniques with books, tapes and training courses.

   ⑤　　　④　　　③　　　②　　　①

3. When I learn information I can use to sell, or a new sales technique, I devise practical ways to use it on my next call.

   ⑤　　　④　　　③　　　②　　　①

4. I am aware of the most common objections to my product and the most effective responses.

   ⑤　　　④　　　③　　　②　　　①

5. I hold regular brainstorming sessions alone or with a group.

   ⑤　　　④　　　③　　　②　　　①

6. I know how to listen and communicate effectively with prospects and use visuals to reinforce my main points.

   ⑤　　　④　　　③　　　②　　　①

Your Total _____

Your Final Score: Add your score for each question to get your final score. If you scored:

From 25 to 30 points: You would've been a star player on Patterson's sales team. For continued improvement, use the ideas from your brainstorming sessions to pioneer your own new sales strategies.

From 18 to 24 points: Never underestimate the value of training — even veterans need it. Have your manager select several sales books, and study them to refresh your memory of basic sales techniques and introduce you to new ones.

Below 18 points: Your sales are slipping through the huge gaps in your training. Seek basic training from a professional, and once you learn how to sell your product, let prospects know about it with creatively designed flyers, brochures and other promotional pieces. Continue to read and learn, and try to perfect a new skill every week or month.

OLYMPIC GOLD MEDALIST MARY LOU RETTON

SHARES HER ENTHUSIASM, OPTIMISM AND

DETERMINATION TO HELP YOU SCORE A

PERFECT 10 IN SALES.

PHOTO BY J. GUICHARD/SYGMA

Mary Lou Retton

I n 1981 no one outside her hometown of Fairmont, West Virginia, even knew her name. By the summer of 1984 she was the most famous girl in America – possibly in the world. Her guts-to-glory story still sends chills down the spine and deserves retelling. Its inspirational message has become a public domain classic. And what about the girl-next-door who could be your sister, cousin, best friend – Mary Lou Retton? The famous grin says it all. Though many might assume that success is a constant downhill ride with all the bumps smoothed out and no hard knocks in the engine, that's far from reality.

Although Mary Lou had gone full bore for two solid years getting ready to face her long shot at Olympic gold, she had no time to savor the moment after she won. Whisked to L.A. for talk show appearances twice in one week, her trip back home more a triumphal march than a restful visit to bask in the warmth of family love, Mary Lou found her life irrevocably altered and there was nothing she could do but accept the inevitable. She belonged to the world now, so she might as well serve its needs.

And that's exactly what this 24-year-old diminutive package of motivational dynamite has done.

Rather than dwell on past glories that she can't hope to recapture, she uses them as teaching tools to spur others on to achieving their potential – whatever it might be.

"I try to look at every situation with a positive attitude," Retton explains. "I don't go into situations thinking maybe or probably. I go into it thinking I'm going to do it." Although she admits that it's difficult to teach that determina-

---

fascinating fact

In her "Retton Vault," Mary Lou adds a full twist to the standard Tsukahara (layout somersault with a full twist) and sails 14 feet through the air.

tion, Retton also finds ways to help people relate to how she found the determination to face almost insurmountable odds.

"I think you've gotta have that determination, that will, that desire to set a goal within you. I tell people you've got to take risks. You've got to ask questions. Only a question that isn't asked is a stupid question. All somebody can say is 'No.' Then you try again. If I'd quit gymnastics every time I fell off beam, I'd never have made it to the Olympics. Never. I tell people you have to seize that moment. When you have a chance to make that sale or win a competition, you have to take that chance."

No risk, no possibility. But along with risk, there's pain. In Retton's determination to live her dream out to its fullest, she gave up everything a young girl treasures. Family life, chatting on the phone, school, dating, proms, homecoming, free time, lifelong friends and the security of staying in your own house, in your hometown, with your own family.

"I spent my whole life preparing for the Olympics. You must prepare for anything you want to accomplish," Retton admits. "My coach, Bela, would have us physically prepared. We would do routines and routines, over and over. It was very repetitive in workouts but we were so ready physically that mentally we were 100 percent confident."

That confidence doesn't just waltz into your life. Nothing replaces skill. On sales calls, the prepared professional knows what's coming, what the objections might be, when to listen and when to speak. The prepared professional never walks into a prospect or customer's office without all the facts, figures, product information, competitive data and the skill to open, present and close. To do any less – to rely on flash and fast talk – is to ask for defeat before the starting gun goes off. Even if it's your very first sale, prepare, prepare and prepare again.

FIRST TIME FOR EVERYTHING

"Salespeople who have never made a sale have the best advantage in the world," declares Retton. "At my first big international meet, I was an alternate. One of our American gymnasts got hurt. And my coach came to me that night and told me that I had to compete the next morning. There were a lot of reasons for me to be nervous. This was my first meet ever to compete against the Russians, Rumanians and Germans. But, I reasoned, there's always going to be that first time. If I messed up, who would notice? I was a last-minute substitute and these people had no idea who I was. But if I did well, and took advantage of the situation and did the best job that I possibly could, it would open huge doors. So, for rookies to really make that break they've got to seize that moment."

Special moments come and go, but professionals can always depend on competition to drive their performance. Without competition, we all would become mediocre. Competition keeps you going one step further and that's the only way to get ahead.

"Competition is wonderful," says Mary Lou. "It only makes you better. I remember if I slacked off a little in the gym, I wouldn't be the best because we had such talented students."

Today, looking at the steady gaze and bright, ready grin, it's easy to forget

---

In gymnastics or in sales, you often live up to your expectations. To face every challenge with the right attitude, Mary Lou Retton recommends preparation, visualization and positive thinking. With these three keys to optimism, you can hope for the best — and get it.

Preparation — Preparation hones your skills and gives you the confidence critical to success. "I spent my whole life preparing for the Olympics," Retton says. "Workouts were repetitive but we were so ready physically that mentally we were 100 percent confident." Rehearse your presentation over and over for managers and co-workers, making at least one new improvement each time.

Visualization — Closing big sales seems easier if you can see yourself doing it. "I used a lot of visualization in gymnastics," Retton maintains. "If I were going on sales calls, I would rehearse what I planned to say before the call. Anticipate prospect responses and be prepared for a variety of situations and answers." Give

achievement
LESSONS

your mental images detail, and review them often to help make the actual call feel more familiar.

Positive thinking — Since thoughts affect performance, focus on the probability of success instead of the possibility of failure. "I try to look at every situation with a positive attitude," Retton says. "I don't go into situations thinking maybe or probably. I go into them thinking I'm going to do it." Send yourself uplifting messages before a call, and replay past successes to boost your confidence.

that just beneath the surface, Mary Lou Retton is one resolute lady. "In my athletic career I learned discipline. Bela taught us never to go into something 50 percent or halfway. When we were working out and doing routines in the gym, when we were very tired and very sore, we had to pretend that we were at the Olympics and give it 110 percent. So I try to do that still. Every speech I give, every appearance I do, I'm trying to motivate them and to make it personal."

Perhaps salespeople need to know what turns up their heat and makes them want to go for the glory. If it's sports videos, watch them. If it's training films, get some. If it's actual body contact sports, join a team. Whatever makes you grab for the brass ring, you have to know you're worth it, that you want it, and how you can motivate yourself to get it.

fascinating fact

When Mary Lou was four years old her mother nicknamed her "The Great Table Smasher and Lamp Toppler."

PATRIOTIC GAMES

Retton made her name a household word at a particular time in history. As she tells it, "I think people are very proud when the Olympics come around. That's something that makes the Olympics so special. You're not just representing a high school or university or even a city with some of the pro teams. You're representing a whole country. I remember in L.A. the whole city was wearing red, white and blue. It was U.S.A. everywhere, flags waving. Part of my success in '84 was that I was the first American ever to win a gold medal in the all-around in gymnastics. I looked at my idols and they either came from the Soviet Union, Rumania or Germany...and finally someone who was born, raised and trained in the United States showed that we could do it, too. I think it opened a lot of people's eyes."

Retton's journey to immortality was a one-in-a-billion shot. A star lit up in her heaven for a fraction of an instant. When you think about it, she trained for nine grueling years, two with arguably the best and most demanding women's gymnastics coach in the world, for four seconds of performance on one event that clinched the gold for her by five one-hundredths of a point.

Does she have a weakness? "Sure," she says. "I'm very emotional and I have a tendency to talk a little too much. I'm a very sensitive person. If there are a thousand articles that come out about me that are positive, and one is negative, that hurts me and I dwell on it and I shouldn't. I have to teach myself – and it's a lesson everyone needs to learn – that you cannot please everybody and not everyone is going to like you. And not everyone is going to agree with what you have to say or with what you believe in."

Taking her fame and fortune in stride, Retton shows the champion within by putting her fate in the hands of a higher authority.

"I feel that God has a plan for me. No one could have written my story better than the reality. Peaking at the right time; the Olympics falling right here in America; coming down to the last event where I was ending on my strongest event – vault; and having to score a perfect 10 and doing it. I'm a very fortunate young lady."

Before hard work, a positive attitude and an expectation that success will come your way, you must define what success means to you. For Retton it's having a goal and then "doing everything possible to make that goal come true. Seeing your way through adversity, going through pain, sacrificing a whole lot, and finally achieving that goal. That is my definition."

Whether success means being an Olympic champion or making a sale, the sacrifice is an absolutely necessary part. "I think it's sweeter when you have made sacrifices for it because when you are sacrificing – and in my case it was literally my childhood – well it was hard at the time, but look what I've accomplished," Retton says.

MAKE YOURSELF UNCOMFORTABLE

Many salespeople work long hours to try to land accounts that never materialize. How does Retton deal with all the elements that are out of her control that conspire to bring her down? "Simple," she says. "You've got to take your chances and not be afraid to fail. You have to push yourself, especially when you're sick or tired or sick and tired of doing what you're doing. I talk in my speech about comfort zones. We all live our lives in comfort zones, avoiding risky situations, avoiding the potential to fail. It's real safe for us. But in order to get ahead of your competition, you've got to go out of your comfort zone. Now your comfort zone is something that you live your whole day, your whole life in. You go to work and do what has to be done to get by. You've got to try to do more. Try that little new thing, that different approach. Get out of your comfort zone and see if it works. It may, it may not, but you'll never know if you don't try.

fascinating fact

At age seven, Mary Lou abandoned tap and ballet lessons to devote herself exclusively to gymnastics.

"I think we all know what our comfort zones are. I think everybody has things they're afraid of and they'll never conquer that fear unless they just take the step. Teamwork is a very useful tool. You can really help one another to step beyond your limits as individuals and as a team.

"I say that T-E-A-M is an acronym. T for together, E for everyone, A for achieves and M for more. A strong team helps everybody individually. A manager who sees a team member in a comfort zone, and sees resistance to getting out of that comfort zone, has an obligation to continue pushing for the good of the team and for the good of the individual. It may take a year or two years. It may take a week or a couple of months. It will be different for each person. But help them to come out of that comfort zone. Show them that it's OK to step out of their normal bounds."

And stay true to yourself. "A lot of salespeople think they have to change personality for the person or the company they're calling on," she muses. "I think a salesperson should definitely be who he or she is.

"You've got to find your own strengths and capitalize on them. My strengths in gymnastics were speed and power. At the time, all the other gymnasts were pretty and balletic and slender and flexible. That was the stereotype before I came onto the scene. But I capitalized on my strengths. You would never see me doing a floor routine to violin music with ballet moves. That wouldn't have been me. So you've got to identify your strengths, develop them and capitalize on them and then use them to your advantage. You've got to use what you have even though you may go into a situation where they were looking for something else to begin with. Definitely."

Play your best card and develop it to its maximum potential. Stress your strengths and make them stronger. The turtle won the race through perseverance. The hare lost through carelessness and ego. The two forces that can help build a success foundation – competition and cooperation – also spur growth.

"I think that positive energy circulates," Retton says. "If you go into a situation with a lot of energy, a good message and a good product, you've got to convince people that they need you and your product, that they want this and that they can't live without it. I really believe that if you're completely prepared, you will accomplish that.

"If you go into a sales meeting feeling 'Well, I'm not sure,' or you're a little shaky, people will sense that, absolutely. Now how can people learn to have that positive attitude? Well, you can tell people how important it is to look at the glass as half full rather than half empty, but they've got to want to believe that. Especially today, people seem to be feeling that everything is beyond their control – hopeless. But they forget that what happens in their lives is ultimately in their own hands. I would just tell people, 'You personally can make a difference.' It may be a tiny little part that they have to offer, but I think that each tiny little part makes a whole big lot of difference. But everybody has to try just a little harder, do just a little better, think just a little deeper, work just a little longer."

NO REST FOR THE WINNER

After her incredible win at the '84 games, Retton went on a whirlwind ride through every temptation she had shunned during her training years. Reporters wanting to interview her, corporations wanting to hire her, endorsement offers from every corner of the globe, a red Corvette as a prize, magazine covers, trips to the White House, autograph hounds and a life that no longer had any corner for privacy – all this for a 16-year-old girl from a small, coal mining town in West Virginia.

But it didn't turn her head for more than an instant. Within a few months after her victory, she was back at the Karolyi gym in Houston to train for the McDonald's Cup. No gymnast had ever come off an Olympic gold coup and gone on to prepare for another big meet, much less win it. But Mary Lou Retton wasn't just another gymnast. She was – and is – a very special lady who

action
PLAN

Mary Lou's 13 Tips
For Success

1. Keep your focus clear.

2. Expect successful outcomes.

3. Capitalize on your strengths.

4. Expect to work hard.

5. Don't dwell on your weaknesses.

6. Seek out competition to improve your performance.

7. Prepare for everything you want to accomplish.

8. Get out of your comfort zone.

9. Stay in overall good condition.

10. Look at every situation with a positive attitude.

11. Visualize perfection and visualize correction.

12. Meet the challenge in tough situations.

13. Develop discipline and determination.

sticks to her principles and her commitment. She thought about it, trained for it and won.

To create a success circle, Retton suggests starting off with small goals. "Work hard to get your first one then go on to the next. Keep your focus clear. When I was seven my dream was to be in the Olympics but it didn't become a reality until I was older, until I was good enough to make the team. I began by moving up from class 3 to class 2 then moving from class 2 to class 1 and then to elite and maybe my next goal was to win the regional competition. And then the nationals and then, of course, the Olympics.

"I think people should set smaller goals for themselves first, achieve those and then move on to bigger and better things. Just because I accomplished my lifetime goal at age 16 doesn't mean I'm going to stop. I'd like to run some gymnastics camps or have a gymnastics school someday. I want to be a mother someday. I have a whole list of things I'd like to do."

To make those goals a reality Retton uses techniques that include visualization. "I used a lot of visualization in gymnastics. If I were going on sales calls, I would definitely go through the approach or what the salesperson plans to say before the call. Do it at home. Do it in front of the mirror. Be prepared to take a different tack if things don't go as expected on the call," Retton suggests. "Anticipate what you think the prospect will say to you and be prepared for a variety of situations and answers.

"Be prepared to stay flexible in the situation. In your visualization, prepare for all possibilities, even the possibility that the sale might not go well. But assume that it will go well. Always prepare yourself for a perfect 10. When I visualized myself going through a beam routine, I didn't imagine myself falling. I visualized myself on the beam – perfect. Always picture it perfect. But I would also picture myself on beam, which is not my strongest event, if I was off a little bit – and we're talking about a quarter of an inch – and if you are off just that little bit it can throw your whole routine off and you could fall – I would visualize how I was going to make myself stay on the beam. I would find myself tucking my stomach in, squeezing my bottom and making sure I was very tight. So always visualize yourself doing the perfect 10 or the best that you possibly can be – which is getting that sale. But also visualize what you can do if something does go wrong. That's IF."

Visualize perfection and also visualize correction. Be prepared to save the situation. Stay on your toes. Be alert for danger signals and respond to them immediately. To do even a little better, to raise your sights and your sales, begin with your motivation to succeed.

> ## fascinating fact
>
> *Mary Lou won the gold medal in Los Angeles by only five one-hundredths of a point.*

"First a salesperson has to want to achieve more," Retton claims. "He may have to stay longer at the office, do more work, sacrifice a little bit more. But if he truly wants it, he'll get it. I truly believe that. My coach used to tell me: 'The harder you work, the luckier you get.'

"I can remember working out. There were probably four to seven girls who would actually be working in Bela's group. If we had even one negative girl in our group, that would bring the whole group down. One person can really put a big black cloud over you. So I try to surround myself with positive people."

What do positive people like? "I really think positive people like a challenge," says Retton. "When things get tough, don't run as you expected, that's a challenge. The positive person will approach the situation with the attitude 'Here's an opportunity. I'll make the most of it.'

"A positive attitude is like a blanket that warms you from inside, that keeps you warm in cold times. When those cold times come, you can rise to the competitive occasion and meet the challenge. For example, during the summer games this year, I'm going to be covering the games for *USA Today*. This paper has a daily circulation of six or seven million. And people ask me: 'Have you done this before?' and I say: 'No.' And they say: 'Oh my gosh, aren't you scared? Aren't you afraid what people will think?' Well, no, I'm looking at it as a challenge. I've never done it before. I want to try it. I'm excited about it. Let's give it a try."

CORCHING WITH CLASS

The coach's crucial role doesn't escape this seasoned veteran of intense competition. "Although I'm a very motivated person," Retton says, "my coach also motivated me to reach inside to get that last drop of energy. With all the pressure and the situation the way it was at the Olympics, he really motivated me to accomplish my goals. I can remember him saying to me: 'Mary Lou, it's now or never. I want to see what you can do. The best vault that you can do.' And that just psyched me up and I said, 'All right. I'm gonna do it!'

"A good coach is number one a good motivator. A good coach works with each individual on the team in the way that person needs. Bela knew how to coach me. When I wasn't doing well in workouts, maybe not making the correction he wanted me to make, he would ignore me. Not so much yell at me but just ignore me. Because he knew that would eat me up. I strove for his attention and discipline.

> ### fascinating fact
>
> *By age 12, Mary Lou Retton was the only elite-level gymnast in West Virginia.*

"My teammate, Julianne McNamara – the two of us trained together six months before the Olympics – was a very shy and timid person. Bela would be extremely gentle with her, never yelling, never raising his voice. A good coach or teacher finds those qualities within a person and brings them out and works with those qualities. Bela's wife, Martha, is as good a coach as Bela but she doesn't like the limelight or cameras at all. When I went to Karolyi's I was not very good on beam at all. She really worked with me and turned me around.

"I can honestly say that at the Olympics, balance beam won me my all-around title. I knew I could do the other three events, but I also knew that I had to stay on beam. And by gosh when I got there she had me prepared. Her style of coaching was in the quiet preparation and in the repetition – doing it over and over and over. Bela and Martha believe that workouts are just like the competition. We would do full routines, with a mount and a dismount. We did not work just on separate parts of a routine – just a turn or a flip – because when you get into the competition, you can't say: 'OK, Judge, watch this little beauty of a flip.' You do the full routine. And that's something they really embedded in my mind.

"So, in sales, if you have trouble asking for the order, don't just practice that. Practice the whole sales call and then ask for the order so it's part of a whole and not just out of context.

"The work ethic, discipline and determination they taught me at the gym have really carried over. I expect to work hard to achieve anything."

What keeps her going? "The motivation to succeed should last all your life. Finding something in the job you're doing that is worthwhile and meaningful to you creates motivation. New challenges keep motivation fresh. So come up with new ideas, develop new accounts, seek out new people and maybe do some cold calling. Reach out to new areas where you haven't sold before. Be bold. Step out of your comfort zone." ▣

Benchmarking
YOUR SUCCESS

Talent alone doesn't win gold medals. Mary Lou Retton had the physical ability to win, plus the determination and spirit that separate good athletes from great ones. To develop the right mix of motivational ingredients in yourself — motivation, preparation, willingness to sacrifice, positive thinking, etc. — take the benchmark test below and use the results to make a positive change.

⑤**=Always,** ④**=Often,** ③**=Sometimes,** ②**=Rarely,** ①**=Never**

1. I prepare for sales calls until I know my presentation and can answer objections easily and thoroughly.

⑤　　④　　③　　②　　①

2. I try unusual sales techniques and call on difficult prospects even though I may fail.

⑤　　④　　③　　②　　①

3. I compete with others on my sales team or at least with my own past performance.

⑤　　④　　③　　②　　①

4. I play up the strong points in my performance and work to improve on my weaknesses.

⑤　　④　　③　　②　　①

5. I set short-, medium- and long-term goals to establish a pattern of growth and improvement.

⑤　　④　　③　　②　　①

6. Before my sales calls, I visualize myself making a terrific first impression, giving a compelling presentation and closing the sale.

⑤　　④　　③　　②　　①

Your Total _____

Your Final Score Add your score for each question to get your final score. If you scored:

From 25 to 30 points: Mary Lou would be proud. You're taking measures to ensure continued growth and success. Remember to keep learning and resetting your goals for ongoing improvement.

From 18 to 24 points: You know what to do, but you need to be more consistent. If you're scared to step outside your comfort zone, make the transition gradual. Know that you are capable of success and remind yourself of its benefits often.

Below 18 points: You have a lot of untapped potential! Instead of practicing some success techniques some of the time, gradually incorporate all of them into your strategy. For each quiz question, write down one action step you can take to improve in that area, then team up with your manager to monitor your progress.

BASIC TRAINING FROM STORMIN' NORMAN

ON DEVELOPING DISCIPLINE, COMMUNICATING

EFFECTIVELY AND SETTING GOALS TO

BECOME A FOUR-STAR SUCCESS.

PHOTO BY THEO WESTENBERGER/GAMMA LIAISON

General Norman Schwarzkopf

A commander in every sense of the word, General H. Norman Schwarzkopf commands attention, respect, loyalty, dedication to duty, adherence to a plan and, most important, the love of the people who serve under him. Without that, no leader can make people perform up to maximum capability.

In this exclusive *Selling Power* profile of one of the great leaders of our age, readers will learn how Schwarzkopf developed his leadership style, implements plans that succeed and motivates people to follow his directives.

Two years ago, few Americans outside the military had ever heard of General H. Norman Schwarzkopf. At that time, the four-star general earned only $113,000 a year heading a small, noncombat planning staff. A year later, the Gulf War offered Schwarzkopf a chance to lead American troops to victory. In the process he earned himself a permanent place of honor in the history books of the world.

After the war, he received countless honors, including a New York City ticker-tape parade, an honorary knighthood from the Queen of England, the Medal of Freedom, and a standing ovation from a joint session of Congress. He has

> ## fascinating fact
>
> *As a youth in Germany, Norman Schwarzkopf was nicknamed "Cuddles" by a group of friends.*

signed on with Bantam Books with an advance of over $5 million for his memoirs; he is one of America's hottest speakers, commanding between $50,000 and $80,000 for each appearance. Although he claims to be politically independent, some analysts predicted that at the close of the Gulf War, had Schwarzkopf chosen to run, the 1992 Democratic presidential ticket would have been his for the taking.

General H. Norman Schwarzkopf is intelligent (170 IQ), a charismatic leader and a superb salesman. No matter how you may feel about the military, when you meet him, he commands your respect, but at the same time gives you the urge to invite him to join your bowling team.

In this article, we'll examine four of his key qualities that anyone can emulate to achieve greater success.

THE POWER OF DECISIONS

As the commander of the United States forces in the Persian Gulf, General H. Norman Schwarzkopf knew that the safety of his troops depended on the quality of his strategic decisions. In his first detailed briefing on the decisive battle plan, Schwarzkopf said that the Iraqis had more tanks, more artillery and more troops in place. "In order to attack a position that is heavily dug in and barricaded, such as the one we had here," he explained, "you should have a ratio of five to one in the way of troops in favor of the attacker." To win the battle, Schwarzkopf had to come up with some way to make up the difference.

He first decided to take out the Iraqi Air Force. Next he developed an ingenious plan of deception. He ordered the United States Marines to prepare a massive amphibious landing along Kuwait's coast under the ominous code name "Imminent Thunder." While Iraq's forces were bracing for an attack from the coast, Schwarzkopf shifted more than 300,000 United States Army troops, complete with 60 days of ammunition and supplies, to positions far

fascinating fact

Norman Schwarzkopf married Brenda Holsinger, a TWA flight attendant from Timberville, Virginia.

west of Kuwait, more than 300 miles from the coast.

Schwarzkopf told the press, "We did what could best be described as the Hail Mary play in football. When the quarterback is desperate for a touchdown at the very end, he steps up behind the center and, all of a sudden, every single one of his receivers goes way out to one flank and they all run down the field as fast as they possibly can and into the end zone. Then he lobs the ball."

With the Iraqi forces pinned into position in the east, Schwarzkopf decided to launch a massive attack led by the First and Second Marine Divisions from the west to break through the Iraqi barrier. In the press briefing the following day, Schwarzkopf proudly stated, "I can't say enough about the two Marine divisions. If I use words like brilliant, it would really be an underdescription of the absolutely superb job that they did in breaching the so-called impenetrable barrier."

Reflecting on his plan, Schwarzkopf told reporters, "I got to tell you, when I insisted on this deception plan with a lot of my commanders, I got a lot of guff. OK. They thought that Schwarzkopf had lost his mind...they fought me all the way."

On the field of battle and in the customer's office, self-sacrifice yields success. Just as military leaders must act in their troops' best interests, salespeople must act in their customers' best interests. When you learn Norman Schwarzkopf's lessons in self-sacrifice, you can win more customers by showing them they come first no matter what.

Care for your customers. In Vietnam, Schwarzkopf risked life and limb to rescue soldiers from a minefield. Your customers should be able to count on you to save them from bad buying decisions, even if that means a smaller sale — or no sale — for you. Before you advise your buyers or close a sale, make sure their success and well-being are your top priority.

Exercise self-discipline. At an early age, Schwarzkopf's father taught him the importance of self-discipline. With it, we can sacrifice today's instant gratification in favor of tomorrow's long-term success. Be aware of the things that tempt you to put off what you know you should do, and devise a plan to help you exercise greater control.

achievement LESSONS

Take courage. Despite the threats to his own life, Schwarzkopf often had to set his fear aside to do his job. Even when you feel intimidated by a buyer or afraid to make your presentation, to win the sale you must deny yourself the luxury of indulging your fear. Prepare yourself for stressful situations with positive visualization and other anxiety-reducing techniques.

Yet Schwarzkopf knew that good leadership depends on sticking with good decisions, no matter what. He later commented on the agonizing process to arrive at the decision: "I thought about this plan every waking and sleeping moment. I would get up every morning and say, 'Let's go back and review the plan.' There were some days when I would get up and would say, 'Oh, it's never going to work and we're going to lose everybody.' And there were other days when I got up and said, 'It's looking pretty good but what else can I do, what else can we modify, what else can we change?' But there comes a point where you can overdo that...You say, OK, that's it! It's frozen. I'm not going to change another damn thing."

THE POWER OF LEADERSHIP

Dr. Abraham Zaleznik, professor emeritus of leadership at Harvard Business School and the author of *The Managerial Mystique: Restoring Leadership in Business*, told the *Los Angeles Times* that the Gulf War taught American business a valuable lesson, "Set clear goals and stick to them." Zaleznik cited the Chrysler Corporation which invested billions of dollars in such unrelated businesses as the corporate jet manufacturer Gulfstream while starving its auto plants. "What were the auto workers on the plant floors supposed to think about Chrysler's goals?" Zaleznik asked.

In a recently released video titled *Take Charge!* retired General Schwarzkopf tells his audience that the multinational forces in Saudi Arabia had rallied together to achieve one single goal: "Kick Saddam Hussein out of Kuwait!"

But good leadership goes far beyond stating clear goals. Schwarzkopf deeply cared for his troops and did everything he could to ensure their welfare. The French magazine *L'Expansion* attributed one of the keys to his success to treating his troops as if they were his customers. He knew that in order for them to execute his commands, he had to deliver the proper equipment and supplies – on time – to the right place, not just one time, but every time.

What sets Schwarzkopf apart from other leaders? He is willing to risk his own life to help the people who have been ordered to follow his command. According to Army reports, on May 28, 1970, while Schwarzkopf was a lieutenant colonel and commander of the First Battalion of the Sixth Infantry Brigade in Vietnam, one of his captains and a lieutenant leading a patrol had been badly wounded in a minefield. Before anyone else could get to the men, Schwarzkopf and his artillery liaison officer, Captain Bob Trabbert, reached the field in their helicopter. Schwarzkopf immediately made an effort to calm down the soldiers and lead them out of the minefield.

As they started moving, one of the soldiers, just a dozen yards away from Schwarzkopf, stepped on a mine which exploded, tearing his right leg apart and wounding both Schwarzkopf and Trabbert. The soldier screamed for help while Schwarzkopf carefully inched his way forward. As he reached the soldier, he reassured him and called Trabbert for a splint. A moment later, a man next to Trabbert set off another mine, killing two soldiers and seriously wounding Trabbert. Schwarzkopf received a Silver Star Medal for the rescue of his soldiers, but, more important, this dramatic experience earned him the reputation as a leader who cares, deep down in his heart, about every one of his followers.

> **fascinating fact**
>
> *General Norman Schwarzkopf has no first name – only the first initial "H."*

THE POWER OF DISCIPLINE

"I am disappointed that the schools are not teaching discipline," explained Schwarzkopf to a reporter. "The type of discipline I am talking about is self-discipline more than enforced discipline." Schwarzkopf added, "I personally believe that discipline is learned in three places: in church, in the home and in the school. And I think those are the three places where a dedication to something higher than service to yourself is instilled."

It was Schwarzkopf's father who planted the idea of discipline in young Norman's mind. He taught the Schwarzkopf children to give up their seats on the bus to the elderly, regardless of race. He taught discipline simply by expectations and example. On his 10th birthday, H. Norman Schwarzkopf received a note from his father stating prophetically, "The success of our lives will be written by your deeds." He also received an antique Persian battle-ax as a sym-

action PLAN

1 Clarify your communication. Great debater and orator Schwarzkopf inspired his troops and won the public's trust with his straight talk and eloquence. When you can move buyers with your words, you stand a much better chance of closing them. Before you speak, consider what you want to say, how you want to say it and who you're talking to to make yourself more convincing.

2 Make a decision. With indecision comes inaction, so you won't find Norman Schwarzkopf sitting on the fence for long. Write down the pros and cons of your important decisions, consider the consequences of each option, then move forward and take action.

3 Strategize for success. To coordinate the efforts of so many people during Operation Desert Storm, Schwarzkopf painstakingly planned his attack. Every buyer and sales call is different, so you need to formulate a customized strategy for each one. Be sure you understand each of your prospect's unique needs and how those needs affect the way you sell.

bolic gift for success in the battle of life.

Self-discipline is a lifelong challenge. It's especially important, though, when things go wrong. Schwarzkopf told reporters, "I do not get mad at people; I get mad at things that happen; I get mad at betrayal of trust; I get angry at a lack of consideration for the soldiers." Yet, as any good leader must, Schwarzkopf manages to stay in control.

He went on to explain, "And contrary to what's been said, I do not throw things. If somebody happens to be in my burst radius when I go off, I make very sure they understand it's not them I'm angry at. Having said that, anytime a guy who's 6-foot-3, weighs 240 pounds and wears four stars loses his temper, everybody runs for cover. I recognize that, but I don't think I'm abusive. There's a difference."

Schwarzkopf has successfully managed one of the toughest challenges with self-discipline any executive has to face – remaining within the boundaries of the guidelines set by higher authorities. During an interview with David Frost, the general hinted that President Bush reined him in when Schwarzkopf wanted to continue the war. Schwarzkopf said, "That was a very courageous act on the part of the President, to also stop the offensive. You know, we didn't declare a cease-fire. What we did was to suspend offensive operations. Frankly, my recommendation had been to continue the march. We had them in a rout and we could have continued to reap great destruction upon them." According to *The New York Times*, the President and the general talked the next day on the telephone and Schwarzkopf reportedly said in complete support of President Bush, "It was a very humane decision."

While self-discipline earns respect in dealing with

people at all levels, when applied to work, it leads to high quality. When *Publisher's Weekly* asked Schwarzkopf about his new book, he replied, "What's always been important to me is that this book be a good book. I realize there's a lot of interest in the subject matter right now, but I would like it to be a book that could still be read 100 years from now."

THE POWER OF COMMUNICATION

An old instruction manual at General Electric outlining the principles of well-focused communication suggests that communicators ask three fundamental questions:

1. What do you want to say?

2. Who are you talking to?

3. How do you want to say it?

In dozens of televised interviews, General Schwarzkopf spoke his mind candidly, honestly and directly. In his speech to Congress, he stirred the emotions of the entire nation. TV cameras caught even his most outspoken critics jumping up first to applaud his words. But Schwarzkopf's communication power goes far beyond eloquence and his superb command of the English language. Many times when he spoke to his troops, Schwarzkopf's message, like a bouquet of flowers, transcended logic and aimed straight at the heart.

> ## fascinating fact
>
> *After 35 years of military service, Norman Schwarzkopf resigned on August 30, 1991.*

One of his teachers, Major General Milton H. Medenbach, who was commandant of cadets at Valley Forge, remembered Schwarzkopf as a bright student: "He could talk on and on about anything," which made him the debating champ of his class.

TV Guide wrote about Schwarzkopf's abilities as a communicator: "He was blunt and direct; he handled the reporters' questions with aplomb, skillfully switching from humor to hardball and back again."

One of his former bosses, Major General Richard Cavazos, told a reporter how Schwarzkopf drove his message home without injuring egos in the process: "He was able to identify weaknesses in his units and correct them without running over his subordinates. He never overreacted, never pounced on them."

Ironically, the Gulf War might have been avoided altogether if Iraqi Foreign Minister Tariq Aziz had studied the art of communication the way Schwarzkopf did. Like Saddam, he consistently misread America's resolve to get Iraq out of Kuwait. On January 9, 1991, U.S. Secretary of State James Baker handed Tariq Aziz an envelope with the presidential seal containing a direct message from George Bush to Saddam Hussein. After reading a copy of the letter, Aziz arrogantly stated, "I cannot receive this letter. The language in this letter is not compatible with language between heads of state." After a lengthy meeting between the two delegations, Saddam's half brother reportedly phoned Baghdad with this message, "The Americans don't want to fight, they want to talk their way out. They are weak."

Only eight days later, General Schwarzkopf told his troops, "This morning at 0300 we launched Operation Desert Storm..." As always, he communicated the right balance between logic and emotion to lead his people: "You have trained hard for this battle and you are ready. During my visits with you, I have seen in your eyes a fire of determination to get this job done quickly so that we may all return to the shores of our great nation. My confidence in you is total. Our cause is just! Now you must be the thunder and lightning of Desert Storm. May God be with you, your loved ones at home and our country."

After the war, he sent the first of his front line troops home with the friendly advice to communicate the whole story saying, "I can hear the war stories now. I know what glorious stories they are going to be. It's a story worth telling. But don't forget to tell the whole story." He told them to "give credit to the multinational troops, the Navy, the Air Force, the countless people who have worked as a solid team in this war." He added, fighting back his emotions, "It's hard to say in words how proud I am of you." ▣

> ## fascinating fact
>
> *Before his own children were born, Schwarzkopf staged magic shows for neighborhood kids at his home in Fort Leavenworth, Kansas.*

Benchmarking YOUR SUCCESS

Even if you're never fired upon by your prospects, to sell them effectively you'll need many of the same qualities Norman Schwarzkopf carries into battle. To be sure you're armed with his strong communication skills, self-discipline, decision-making ability and other attributes, take this benchmark quiz. The results will tell you what traits to develop to launch a sales attack your buyers won't want to resist.

⑤=**Always,** ④=**Often,** ③=**Sometimes,** ②=**Rarely,** ①=**Never**

1. Even when I feel like doing other things, I have the self-discipline to make myself do what I know must be done.

       ⑤   ④   ③   ②   ①

2. I use strong communication skills that get my point across concisely and persuasively.

       ⑤   ④   ③   ②   ①

3. I understand the importance of thorough preparation and go into every call confident that I have the knowledge and skill I need to sell effectively.

       ⑤   ④   ③   ②   ①

4. I am willing to sacrifice a sale if I don't think my product is the best choice for my buyer.

       ⑤   ④   ③   ②   ①

5. For each call I make, I devise a customized strategy to maximize my chances of success.

       ⑤   ④   ③   ②   ①

6. I can analyze my decisions and take action on them without spending too much time thinking about them.

       ⑤   ④   ③   ②   ①

Your Total _____

Your Final Score Add your score for each question to get your final score. If you scored:

From 25 to 30 points: You have what it takes to win, and you know how to use it. Just as Schwarzkopf always tries to find out what the enemy is up to, stay on top of your competitors to make your efforts even more effective.

From 18 to 25 points: On sales calls, beware of relying too much on knowledge and ability and not enough on preparation. Also, remember that it's in your best interests to look out for your buyers' best interests, so always do what's best for them. Study a book on self-discipline so you will be less tempted to skip important call preparation steps.

Below 18 points: To make your selling skills work for you you need to work on such other non-selling skills as self-discipline and self-sacrifice. Team up with your manager to analyze your sales performance and uncover the root causes of your problems.

WITH A STRONG SENSE OF DUTY, BETTER

ORGANIZATION AND ONGOING IMPROVEMENT, YOU

CAN FOLLOW IN THE IRON LADY'S FOOTSTEPS AND

PRIME YOURSELF FOR SUPERACHIEVER STATUS.

PHOTO BY JEAN GUICHARD/GAMMA LIAISON

Margaret Thatcher

argaret Thatcher (1) enjoyed more than 11 years in power as the Prime Minister of England, (2) led her nation to war in the Falkland Islands and won a glorious victory, (3) survived a carefully planned assassination attempt, (4) created a new political style named after her, (5) refused to draw a higher salary than her ministers, (6) was the mother of twins, and (7) was raised in a small apartment that only had cold running water, an outside toilet, and no bath. Considered together, these facts begin to paint a picture of one of the most successful women of this century. In this chapter we'll review Margaret Thatcher's success skills and take a close look at her leadership and management principles. As you discover the blueprints to Margaret Thatcher's success, you'll be able to set new standards for your own performance and create higher levels of success for yourself.

> ## fascinating fact
>
> *Margaret Thatcher is the 20th century's longest-serving British Prime Minister.*

A GREENGROCER'S DAUGHTER

Margaret Hilda Thatcher grew up in a small apartment over her father's grocery store in the town of Grantham, located 100 miles north of London. She once told a reporter, "My sister and I were brought up in the atmosphere that you work hard to get on." Their apartment had only cold running water, an outside toilet, and no bath. The store had a post office section and sold groceries, cigarettes, confections and spices.

Her father, Alfred Roberts, was very active in the community. He co-founded the Rotary Club, served on the local town council for 25 years and later became Mayor of Grantham. She described her mother, Beatrice, a trained dressmaker, as "intensely practical," who taught her how to bake bread, make her own clothes and decorate her room.

Margaret Thatcher once reflected on her upbringing: "We were Methodists and Methodist means method. We were taught what was right and wrong in considerable detail. There were certain things you just didn't do and that was that. Duty was very, very strongly ingrained into us."

In school, she was most impressed with her headmistress, Miss Williams. She once told a reporter that Miss Williams was one of the most influential women in her life: "She always said, you must not be too satisfied with what you have done. You must try to do better. Whatever you have, you must try to live up to the best that is within you!" Margaret Thatcher has designed her entire life based on Miss Williams' philosophy of ongoing improvement.

fascinating fact

Thatcher's approval rating rose from 22 percent immediately preceding the Falkland Islands conflict to 59 percent immediately following it.

Politics was often discussed at the dinner table and in the grocery store, and young Margaret felt a natural interest in the subject. She helped in her father's political campaigns, took elocution lessons in school, learned to play the piano, became a member of the debating team and developed her talents in the dramatic arts. Influenced by an enthusiastic chemistry teacher, she elected science as her field of study, but realized later that she'd rather become a lawyer.

In 1943 she was admitted to Sommerville College at Oxford, one of England's oldest women's colleges. She soon joined the Oxford University Conservative Association (the members of England's Conservative Party are called "Tories") where her political ambitions continued to expand. Margaret Thatcher was a great admirer of Winston Churchill and helped in his 1945 election campaign. She canvassed from door to door, handed out leaflets and delivered her first campaign speeches. Her lifetime goal was to make a significant contribution to her country. When Churchill was voted out of office, Margaret Thatcher was disappointed and commented later, "To me it seemed utterly unbelievable that the nation could have rejected Winston after everything he had done."

After graduation she took a job as a research chemist. In 1948 the Oxford Graduate Association sent the 23-year-old Margaret to the annual Conservative Party Conference where she won her first political victory. She was considered as a candidate for a seat in Parliament. In February of 1949 her candidacy was approved by a voice vote by an overwhelming majority. At the reception following the vote she was introduced to a guest who offered to drive her to the train station. His name was Denis Thatcher. He was more than impressed with the youngest woman in England to run for Parliament.

THE THATCHER FAMILY

In December of 1951, Margaret Roberts and Denis Thatcher were married in London. The beaming bride wore a velvet dress of Tory blue. Thirty years later, in a BBC radio interview Margaret Thatcher reflected on her husband, "I was just lucky with Denis. Absolutely marvelous." She told the interviewer that her husband always encouraged her to use her talents.

Soon after their marriage, the young couple moved to London. While Mr. Thatcher ran the family business (a paint and preservatives company), Mrs. Thatcher waged several unsuccessful campaigns against the ruling Labour Party and pursued her legal studies to become a barrister. In early 1953, when she was five months pregnant, she passed her intermediate bar exam. In August she gave birth to twins, a boy and a girl named Mark and Carol. She immediately hired a nanny, continued her studies and passed her final bar exams in December.

As the mother of twins, Margaret Thatcher received a double dose of guilt and worry – guilt for not being with her children to help them through important phases of their development, and worry about their welfare while she was pursuing her career. Many times she worked 16 to 18 hours a day, and often seven days a week.

In an interview with the *Sunday Express*, she explained how she managed to balance family and work: "A married woman who wants to have a full-time job needs to be extremely well organized. She has to be able to deal with domestic affairs quickly, make up her mind about household menus and shopping lists."

In another interview she emphasized the need for reliable help: "It is possible, in my view, for a woman to run a home and continue with her career provided two conditions are fulfilled. First, her husband must be in sympathy with her wish to do another job. Secondly, where there is a young family, the joint incomes of husband and wife must be sufficient to employ a first-class nanny/housekeeper to look after things in the wife's absence. The second is the key to the whole plan. If we couldn't afford to have resident help in the home, I would give up my career tomorrow."

WINNING A SEAT IN THE HOUSE OF COMMONS

Talk is the principal tool of persuasion for salespeople and politicians. Former Prime Minister Harold Macmillan once said, "Mastery of the country begins with mastery of the House of Commons." Anyone who has ever witnessed a debate in the British Parliament will testify that it can be a surprisingly raucous place.

Speakers often get interrupted by boisterous shouts, foot-stomping, fist-banging or impulsive insults. Yet it is the free, uninhibited expression of human thought that advances the ship of state through the uncharted waters of the country's future. Tony Benn, a former leader of the Labour Party's left wing, once commented about Britain's democratic process: "Through talk we tamed kings, restrained tyrants, averted revolution and ultimately reflected public needs in such a way as to help shape public policy."

Margaret Thatcher's communication skills were charismatic. She expressed her thoughts with simple, yet powerful, words and her delivery showed passion and certainty to remove any chance for ambiguity. Her keen intellect often leapfrogged those who were resistant to opening their minds to a more practical

As a schoolgirl, Margaret Thatcher learned that accomplishments should be only a prelude to future achievement. By reaching for ongoing improvement, she rose from obscurity to Britain's highest political office. Even if you're at the top of your game now, remember that others want to take your place. For a long and bright future, strive to improve on your past.

Avoid complacency. As her former headmistress Miss Williams told Thatcher, you must not be too satisfied with what you have done. Be proud of your accomplishments, but don't let pride keep you from pursuing bigger and better goals. Instead, let your current achievements serve as a guide for future success.

achievement LESSONS

Polish your skills. Her speaking skills had already helped Thatcher become the first woman leader of the Conservative Party, but in 1978 she hired a media consultant to strengthen her image even more. She fine-tuned her speeches and toned down her voice for a human touch that made her more persuasive.

Every week, take time to learn a new sales skill or improve an old one.

Take risks. When she challenged her mentor for Conservative Party leadership in 1974, Thatcher knew she was taking a chance. At the same time, she knew risk is necessary to growth. To keep rising through the ranks in sales, be willing to go out on a limb. Not every risk will pay off, but being willing to take risks will.

way of thinking. When asked about her feelings as a woman in a field traditionally dominated by men, she remarked, "It doesn't matter whether you are a man or a woman. What matters is your grasp of the problems and the need for action."

In 1959, after running a well-organized campaign, she was elected Member of Parliament by the district of Finchley. In her maiden speech in February 1960, Margaret Thatcher introduced a bill to force local governments to admit reporters to certain council and committee meetings. At that time she was the youngest of the 25 women in the House of Commons (with a total of 630 members). Her presentation had substance, and soon the bill was approved by the House.

MINISTER THATCHER FAILS FORWARD

After the 1964 election, Labour Party candidate Harold Wilson became Prime Minister. The Conservative Party selected Edward Heath as their opposition leader and Margaret Thatcher was appointed junior spokesperson on housing and land. Later she took on the job of education minister of Heath's shadow government.

In 1970, the political tides turned and Edward Heath became Prime Minister. Margaret Thatcher became the government's secretary of state for education and science. During her first year she made a political mistake that took her by surprise. She gave in to demands for sweeping budget cuts and agreed to end the expensive practice of providing free milk to students in primary schools. When the word leaked out, demonstrators began shouting "Mrs. Thatcher, Milk-Snatcher."

Her political opponents were even more cruel. When she introduced her proposal to Parliament, members of the opposition shouted, "Ditch the bitch!" *The Sun*, a London newspaper, called her "the most unpopular woman in Britain." There was little she could do but grin and bear the wave of adversity and wait until the public focused on more important issues. Margaret Thatcher admitted later that the criticism had hardened her. When asked how she coped she explained, "You have to build an armor around yourself, knowing the things they say aren't true."

CHALLENGING OPPORTUNITY

Soon Edward Heath's government faced the tougher challenges of the oil embargo, record unemployment, a labor strike, rampant inflation and a rapidly weakening currency. The Labour Party continued to gain strength and in 1974 the Conservatives were voted out of office. Margaret Thatcher took on a new role and became environment minister of the shadow government.

To improve its political fortunes, the Conservative Party decided on a new leadership selection process. Margaret Thatcher recognized an opportunity to advance her career and in November of 1974 she informed Edward Heath of her plans to become a candidate for her party's leadership. Challenging her former mentor was a risky move, yet she had faith in her abilities, she was confident in her plans and she trusted her political instincts.

Opinion polls indicated that Thatcher had little chance of winning against the incumbent opposition leader. However, on February 4, 1975, her party cast 130 votes for Margaret Thatcher, while Edward Heath received only 119. Heath resigned immediately. When the second ballot was cast on February 11, Margaret Thatcher became the first woman leader of the

Conservative Party and the leader of the opposition.

Her victory created a wave of enthusiasm in the country and the House of Commons. She quickly scheduled a whirlwind tour to visit seven foreign countries including the United States where she met with President Gerald Ford and Secretary of State Henry Kissinger. To increase her influence on a global level, she delivered many hard-line speeches against Russia's thirst for world dominance and lack of concern for human rights. The Russian news agency TASS called her the "Iron Lady," a label meant to be derogatory, but she wore it with pride, like a medal of honor.

THE LONG ROAD TO POWER

When Harold Wilson unexpectedly stepped down as Prime Minister in November 1975, James Callaghan, a savvy Labour Party member, was elected Prime Minister. As the leader of the opposition, Margaret Thatcher increased her influence on the global scene and sharpened her oratory against the government in power. During Callaghan's term the British economy worsened, unemployment rose, there were more strikes and immigration problems persisted. Yet Thatcher's shadow government appeared to be stuck in the secondary role of talking – without the privilege of taking action.

Although she was able to increase her popularity in the international arena, her image had plateaued in England. She soon took her own advice, "If you do not at first do what you want to do, you just come at it another way and try again." In 1978 she engaged a media consultant to help polish her appearance. Her speeches became more polished and poised. In an effort to become more persuasive she learned to tone down her voice and made greater efforts to allow her human qualities to shine through.

Margaret Thatcher had developed a plan for reforming England and she was prepared to fight for her convictions. After 19 years in the House of Commons, she knew that she was ready to become Prime Minister. In an interview with

> ### fascinating fact
>
> *Thatcher's son, Mark, has been both a race car driver and a Dallas, Texas, auto executive.*

the London *Times* she confessed how much she enjoyed competition: "I must say the adrenaline flows when they really come out fighting at me and I fight back and I stand there and I know: 'Now come on, Maggie, you are wholly on your own. No one can help you.' And I love it."

After several unsuccessful attempts to challenge the party in power, in March 1979 she forced a showdown, delivered a fiery speech and proposed a no-confidence vote. After a seven-hour debate and an inconclusive voice vote, the speaker called for a "division" where the members approving the no-confidence vote leave the chamber to the right-hand lobby and those opposing the motion walk out to the left-hand lobby. When the Speaker announced the vote count, Thatcher's motion had been approved by 311 members and rejected by 310 members. The next day, Prime Minister James Callaghan requested the Queen to dissolve Parliament and national elections were set for May 3, 1979.

fascinating fact

Thatcher had left the bathroom in her Brighton hotel just two minutes before an IRA bomb destroyed it.

Both parties engaged in a tough election campaign and both parties were predicted to win. The campaign themes looked like a role reversal. Margaret Thatcher's Conservative strategy focused on change, reform and renewal, while the Labour Party promised stability. The press was abuzz about the possibility of having a woman as Prime Minister. Margaret Thatcher elegantly sidestepped the issue and reminded her fellow subjects that the British would never have beaten the Spanish Armada if it had not been for the firm hand of Elizabeth I. She canvassed the country with a high level of enthusiasm, determination and discipline. Political observers credited her well-organized campaign as the key to winning the election.

On May 4, at 2:45 p.m., the Conservative victory became official. James Callaghan resigned and Margaret Thatcher asked for the traditional royal audience to formally assume the leadership of the government. After the official meeting with Queen Elizabeth II, she was escorted to 10 Downing Street, the Prime Minister's official residence.

A huge crowd of reporters wanted to get the first reactions to her victory. She recalled her modest background and credited her father for his guidance and wisdom. To herald the Thatcher era of Britain's history, she quoted St.

Francis of Assisi, "Where there is discord may we bring harmony, where there is error may we bring truth, where there is doubt may we bring faith, and where there is despair may we bring hope." It was a tremendous moment for Margaret Thatcher. Only very few privileged people are granted such a glorious experience during their lifetimes.

THE LEADERSHIP STYLE OF THE IRON LADY

Margaret Thatcher's first cabinet meeting set the tone of how she expected her government to run: efficiently, effectively, where people work as a team and where all ministers are expected to play from the same sheet of music.

Within the first three months she began a series of changes that led to lower taxes, lower government spending and fewer government controls. Visiting heads of state like German Chancellor Helmut Schmidt noticed a "spirit of decisiveness" and the British press lauded her for making good on her campaign promises. She quickly became a rising star in international politics. At her first European Heads of Government meeting in Strasbourg, she stole the show as the only woman.

As her circle of international friends widened, her global influence expanded. Before her first seven-nation summit in Tokyo, Russia's Premier Kosygin invited her to an informal stopover in Moscow. During the 90-minute chat, Kosygin served Russian caviar and French champagne hoping to bend her ear on arms limitations and the world economy. Thatcher, however, tried to win his sympathy for Vietnamese refugees.

At the Tokyo summit she left other heads of state impressed with her vast knowledge and quick grasp of the essence of complex problems. She was friendly, yet she kept her distance. She made sure that other heads of state would address her as Madame Prime Minister, not as "Margaret." It took foreign heads of state only one face-to-face meeting to realize that they were dealing with an extraordinary leader. Secretary of State George Schultz described her best: "She's tough and smart. She's a great and determined lady who's shown us what leadership is all about." What made her so remarkable was that she understood how to use power. Margaret Thatcher explained, "All power is a trust. We have to use our power wisely and well."

Throughout her term as prime minister she encouraged her fellow citizens to assume a greater share of individual responsibility and to treasure the gift of independence. In a speech to a group of business leaders she stated, "I came to office with one deliberate intent: to change Britain from a dependent to a self-reliant society; from a give-it-to-me to a do-it-yourself nation; a get-up-and-go instead of a sit-back-and-wait Britain." When the opposition noisily jeered her vision, she often used George Bernard Shaw's famous line in contempt of her colleagues, "Liberty means responsibility. That is why most men dread it." Her philosophies, her personality and her political selling style became even more focused, effective and compelling.

fascinating fact

Under Thatcher's leadership, the number of unionized workers in Britain dropped 25 percent to 9 million by 1987.

A BRUSH WITH DEATH

Margaret Thatcher often used to write her speeches in the wee hours of the morning. She enjoyed the quiet time, which helped her ideas to crystallize. Her high level of energy allowed her to get by on about five hours of sleep.

In October 1984 she stayed with her husband, Denis, in an elegant suite at the Grand Hotel in Brighton, an old seaside resort where the Conservative Party held their annual conference. While most delegates were sleeping, at 2:50 a.m. Margaret Thatcher was still polishing her speech for the next day. At 2:54 a.m. a powerful blast ripped through the building. A carefully hidden bomb exploded four floors above Margaret Thatcher's suite and tore out a huge section of the hotel's facade. The results were devastating. Five people died and 34 people were injured as four stories collapsed one on top of the other. Although the bathroom in Thatcher's suite was destroyed, she and her husband escaped without injury. The Irish Republican Army claimed responsibility for the terrorist attack. They hoped to kill the British Cabinet and threatened more violence in the future.

Margaret Thatcher announced immediately after the bombing, "Life must go on. The conference will go on as usual." She kept her word, and after a short period of rest, she entered the Brighton conference hall at 9:30 a.m. and was received by thunderous applause. She told her audience, "The fact that we are gathered here now – shocked, but composed and determined – is a sign not only that this attack has failed, but that all attempts to destroy democracy by terrorism will fail."

A few months later, Margaret Thatcher admitted that the terrorist attack had given her a new outlook on life saying, "Life is infinitely more precious to me now. When something like that happens, it alters your perspective. You're not going to be worried or complain about silly little things any more." Like many people who have had a brush with death, Margaret Thatcher increased her focus on life saying, "Life is always scary in some respect, but it is also full of hope. In the end your hope rests upon what you are prepared to do to help things along."

RETURNING TO PRIVATE LIFE

Just as many people in England had a hard time understanding the popularity of Ronald Reagan, many Americans were puzzled by England's growing dislike of Margaret Thatcher. After 11 years as the undefeated leader of the British government, people began to question Margaret Thatcher's ability to contribute to further improvement. Students of leadership know that it is human nature to seek out strong leaders, yet once a strong leader is in power, it is equally human to promote new and able leaders to knock the old leader off the pedestal. During her last year in power, opinion polls showed that the Labour Party would beat her and

action PLAN

1 Embrace change. As Prime Minister, Thatcher tried "to change Britain from a dependent to a self-reliant society..." She knew that with change came improvement, and was willing to upset the status quo in favor of something better. What changes can you make to your routines or techniques to take your sales in a new and improved direction?

2 Do your duty. Thatcher's strong sense of responsibility drove her to do what she knew needed to be done. How can you better understand your responsibilities to your buyers, their expectations and how to fulfill those expectations?

3 Shrug off rejection. After she agreed to stop providing free milk to primary school children, the public turned on Thatcher so harshly that she was called "the most unpopular woman in Britain." Thatcher explained that to cope she shielded herself from the criticism, knowing that what was being said about her wasn't true. What can you do to protect yourself from rejection by prospects so that you stay motivated to keep calling on them?

she was seen as "out of touch with ordinary people."

The Bishop of Durham called Mrs. Thatcher's policies "wicked." Oxford law professor Ronald Dworkin claimed, "The very concept of liberty is being challenged and corroded by the Thatcher government." Some newspapers viciously called her "Attila the Hen."

In her own party her management style raised eyebrows since she replaced more ministers than any previous Prime Minister. It was no secret that she expected obedience in her ranks and it was only a question of time until her followers turned into rebels. Sam Rayburn, the U.S. Speaker of the House, was once quoted as saying, "You cannot be a leader, and ask other people to follow you, unless you know how to follow, too." It may be simplistic to say that Margaret Thatcher's iron will created an element of fear that eroded her support. It may be too easy to call inflexibility the chief cause of her fall.

People close to her affirm that more than a decade at the top did not change Margaret Thatcher's basic character. However, her legendary success had given her the appearance of royalty and her name became a trademark of a very distinct brand of political wisdom (Thatcherism).

A new generation of people began to resist her strong medicine for improvement. After $11^{1}/_{2}$ years as Prime Minister, three previous election victories, and a glorious military triumph in the Falkland Islands, Margaret Thatcher told her cabinet, "It's a funny old world, that here I have won a majority of my party, and yet I feel I have to go."

On November 22, 1990, Margaret Thatcher resigned as Prime Minister of England and, without great fanfare, retired to private life. ▣

For 11 years as Prime Minister, Margaret Thatcher had to sell her people on her ability and policies, and earn their trust and loyalty. To do it, she made the most of her ability to overcome setbacks, brush off rejection, embrace change and improve consistently. Your success depends on the same qualities. With the quiz below, find out what you and Thatcher have in common, and take the steps suggested to boost your performance.

⑤=Always, ④=Often, ③=Sometimes, ②=Rarely, ①=Never

1. I am able to keep my accounts, my territory and my time organized for optimum performance.

   ⑤   ④   ③   ②   ①

2. When I notice that I need to strengthen a selling skill, I get the help I need quickly.

   ⑤   ④   ③   ②   ①

3. I believe in myself even when the odds seem against me.

   ⑤   ④   ③   ②   ①

4. I am happy when I close a big sale or meet a goal, but I always keep striving to improve on my past performance.

   ⑤   ④   ③   ②   ①

5. I feel an obligation to do my best for my buyers, and consistently try to exceed their expectations.

   ⑤   ④   ③   ②   ①

6. I see change as necessary to growth, and don't hesitate to alter my techniques or routine when I think I should.

   ⑤   ④   ③   ②   ①

Your Total _____

Your Final Score Add your score for each question to get your final score. If you scored:

From 25 to 30 points: For you, good selling is a personal responsibility. Now that you have the winning attitude, watch out for negative people, information and situations that might bring you down. Also, take enough time for yourself to avoid burnout.

From 18 to 25 points: A low sense of responsibility toward yourself and your buyers may keep you from continuously improving. Today's success doesn't guarantee tomorrow's, so get motivated to do your best for yourself and your buyers with speakers and fiction or nonfiction books and movies that inspire you, or compete with others on your sales team. When you build momentum, you should find it easier to get and stay organized, embrace change and do anything else you need to to reach your goals.

Below 18 points: Before you can succeed, you must believe you're capable of winning. Make sure you have what you need: good training, good prospects and a plan. Think about the messages you send yourself, and make a conscious effort to make them all positive. Do the things that make you feel deserving of success, and you should feel more empowered to earn it.

IF YOU CAN MATCH THIS ATLANTA BRAVE'S

DETERMINATION, CARING AND DESIRE FOR NEW

CHALLENGES, YOUR SALES ARE BOUND TO

TAKE A TURNER FOR THE BETTER.

PHOTO BY THEO WESTENBERGER/GAMMA LIAISON

Ted Turner

For Ted Turner, 1996 was another banner year. By merging his phenomenally successful Turner Broadcasting with global media conglomerate Time Warner, Turner emerged as the largest single Time Warner stockholder, retaining shares valued at about $2.7 billion. He also celebrated the 20th anniversary of TBS Superstation, CNN's 16th year on the air and, on a personal note, five years of marital bliss with actress and fitness queen Jane Fonda. Despite his successes, however, critics continue to nip at Turner's heels. At every step on his roller-coaster ride from outdoor advertising salesman to cable television magnate (with side ventures as America's Cup champion, major league baseball owner and buffalo rancher) the naysayers have predicted Turner's inevitable fall. Just as consistently he has proven them wrong, often surpassing even his own overly optimistic predictions before blithely moving on to the next seemingly insurmountable challenge.

Few would have anticipated Ted Turner's success. He posted only mediocre grades at a high school military academy – while resetting the school's record books for hours spent marching off demerits for his numerous infractions.

Modest academic record aside, Turner's school days offered glimpses of the competitive fire and persistence that would characterize his later successes in the business world. Lacking any real athletic skill, the young Turner eagerly turned his attention to sailing, a sport where he could replace strength and coordination

> **fascinating fact**
>
> *At the McCallie School in Chattanooga, Tennessee, Ted earned more than one thousand demerits during his first year. His classmates voted him "Neatest Cadet."*

with determination, intelligence and skill. His desire to win every race quickly earned Turner the nickname "Turnover Teddy" for his frequent capsizings.

In his high school sailing club Turner was eager to prove that he could sail year-round, causing one teacher to recall that Ted would sail "in weather where no sane human being would ever set foot in a sailboat," according to the Porter Bibb biography *It Ain't As Easy As It Looks*. Turner has explained that his early dedication to excellence stemmed from one singular desire.

"I was interested in one thing," he says in Bibb's book, "and that was finding out what you could accomplish if you really tried. My interest was always in why people did the things they did, and what causes people to rise to glorious heights."

Continuing his competitive ways at Brown, in his sophomore year Turner helped the university sailing team win the prestigious Timme Angston Trophy Regatta in Chicago. To win the regatta's final race, Turner boldly chose to sail across a patch of ice the other boats had skirted. If his boat managed to cross the ice safely, he would gain a pivotal advantage. If not, the consequences could be dire.

Holding their breath, the Brown team pulled up rudder, wobbled across the patch and nearly capsized on the other side. But they made it. With chattering teeth, frozen toes and a boat half-filled with water, the Brown crew triumphantly crossed the finish line and brought home the trophy. The race was quintessential Ted Turner. He was to frequently follow the same pattern facing future challenges, succeeding by using his instincts as a guide, taking bold risks and flouting conventional wisdom.

THE BILLBOARD WONDER KID

Turner returned home to Georgia after his departure from Brown and began work for his father's billboard company, Turner Advertising. A legendary salesman who had turned a small-time outdoor advertising firm into a multimillion-dollar enterprise, Ed Turner cast a considerable shadow. He insisted, however, that his son bring in his share of new customers before being considered for management. Having the good fortune to inherit his father's charm, the younger Turner was more than up to the challenge.

Former Turner Advertising sales rep Hudson Edwards recalled to unauthorized Turner biographer Porter Bibb, "Ted was one of the greatest salesmen in the world. Just like his father. Either one of them could charm a rattlesnake."

In 1960, with new bride and fellow sailing aficionado Judy Nye at his side, the 21-year-old Ted took over Turner Advertising's Macon office, throwing himself into the work with missionary zeal, often logging 15-hour days, seven days a week at the office. His personal credo was "Early to bed, early to rise, work like hell and advertise," and in just two years Turner doubled sales at the Macon office, simultaneously insinuating himself into local business circles.

By 1962 Turner Advertising was doing so well that Ed Turner decided to make the leap into the big time. He decided to acquire the Atlanta, Richmond, Norfolk and Roanoke offices of General Outdoor Advertising, the country's largest billboard company, using money borrowed against General Outdoor's own assets. Turner Advertising would become the largest billboard company in the south.

Ted was ecstatic about the deal, especially after being named assistant general manager of the Atlanta branch, but his father's enthusiasm seemed to dim. Despite all indications that he had landed a plum, Ed Turner slowly began to sink into a deep depression, increasing his already-dangerous binge drinking and chain smoking. Just five months after closing the deal and against his son's objections, the elder Turner resold the new holdings to his business partner, Bob Naegele, for little more than he had paid. Surprising as this turn of events must have seemed to friends and business colleagues, however, a greater shock was yet to come when on March 5, 1963, Ed Turner took his own life.

> ## fascinating fact
>
> *Turner once forced fans at a baseball game to sing "Take Me Out To the Ball Game" three times to get the words right.*

TED AT THE HELM

Ted was devastated by the news of his father's death. Ed Turner left his son money in the bank and what remained of Turner Advertising, but the ambitious

Ted could only be satisfied by recapturing the entire business. Flying out to Palm Springs to confront Naegele, Ted dropped the bombshell that he intended to renege on his father's deal. Naegele had bought the business from Ed more out of friendship than any Machiavellian aims, so he easily acquiesced, even giving Ted five years to come up with the cash to finance the buyback.

At just 24, sitting atop a mountain of debt but thrilled to have his father's company whole again, Ted assumed the task of running Turner Advertising. To his pleasant surprise, Turner discovered that the billboard business practically minted money. While Turner Advertising was thriving, however, all was not rosy at home. Long weary of Ted's mood swings, Turner's wife, Judy, left him after only two years, taking their two children with her.

By the late '60s Turner began growing bored with the day-to-day tedium of running a successful regional billboard company. He started casting around for new challenges and soon set his sights on the broadcasting industry, specifically WAPO, a small-time Chattanooga station. Despite his eagerness to own the station, Turner decided to play it cool and told WAPO's financially strapped owners he needed time to think over the deal.

Before he could make an offer, however, another buyer stepped in and closed a deal. Turner was beside himself. Never one to accept defeat, he wound

Even before he bought the Braves, Ted Turner knew he belonged in the big leagues. His faith in himself and his potential dwarfed any obstacle in his way to help guarantee his ultimate success. Make Turner's experiences a blueprint for building your own confidence to superachiever levels.

Rise to another level. Turner claims that in disputes between VIPs and "little guys," the little guy rises to the VIP's level. When you make calls on important executives, refuse to feel intimidated. Rise to your buyer's level by viewing yourself as equally capable, important and professional.

Take on tough accounts. Even when winning nationwide accounts seemed unlikely, Turner encouraged his WTCG salespeople to try. Believe in your ability to do what no one else has done. Pursue the most difficult and sought-after buyers. With some persistence and ingenuity, you might break new ground.

achievement
LESSONS

Go out on a limb. Ted Turner had the courage to try such risky sales approaches as kissing a prospect's feet. When conventional selling methods fail, have the confidence to try a more unorthodox strategy. Whether it works or not, making the attempt at least gives you a second chance to succeed.

up buying WAPO from the new owner for an additional $300,000 and stock options. Turner learned from the WAPO negotiation never to hesitate over a decision. In future deals of much greater consequence, he would simply decide on the spot. On the heels of WAPO the company acquired another Chattanooga radio station as well as one in Jacksonville and two in Charleston.

Turner also had a unique ability to inspire others to share his dreams. Longtime family financial advisor Irwin Mazo says that it was well nigh impossible to avoid getting caught up in Turner's enthusiasm.

"He could have retired anytime during those early years and never looked back," Mazo told Porter Bibb. "But then we started making acquisitions, always trying to use the other guys' money. That was Ted's genius. He could charm the pants off anybody when he wanted to. Usually the fellow we acquired would turn around and work twice as hard for Ted as he ever had for himself. When Ted made his next move, into radio, it didn't make a lot of sense until you heard Ted explain it. Then, suddenly, we weren't Turner Advertising anymore, we were the Turner Communications Company."

> ## fascinating fact
>
> *Turner owns a $3 million penthouse that rests atop CNN Center in Atlanta.*

TURNER AND TELEVISION

After radio, Turner Communications took the next logical step into the burgeoning television market. When WJRJ, a local Atlanta UHF station, came onto the market, Turner jumped at the chance. Hemorrhaging money at $50,000 a month, and within 30 days of going under, WJRJ appeared to observers as a singularly poor investment for Turner. Even though the station was Atlanta's number-two independent UHF station, WJRJ's internal research showed that only 5 percent of the city's households could even pick up its signal.

Turner ignored the appeals for caution from the company's board of directors and from Mazo, who foresaw the station sinking Turner Communications, and went ahead with the purchase. He considered television merely another means of selling advertising, and advertising was one business he knew well.

For the actual deal, however, Turner did carry an ace up his sleeve. As with the purchase of Outdoor Advertising, Turner reverse-merged Turner Communications with the station's ownership in a tax-free stock swap, exchanging no cash in the process.

Turner wound up in control of the combined company and went public in the process. Without skipping a beat he then turned around and bought another television station, this one in Charlotte, North Carolina, causing Mazo to resign in protest. Turner Communications took on an additional $3 million in debt for the Charlotte station and Turner himself borrowed $250,000 against his signature.

Despite valid criticisms that the company could not afford these deals and that he knew absolutely nothing about the broadcasting business, Turner followed his instincts and forged ahead.

"I love it when people say I can't do something," he is quoted as saying by biographer Robert Goldberg. "There's nothing that makes me feel better, because all my life people have been telling me that I wasn't going to make it."

Turner discovered synergy long before it became a corporate catch phrase: He began using his unsold billboard space to promote his radio and television stations to the public. In television he discovered the practice of counterprogramming, running *Star Trek* reruns and old movies against the networks' news shows and Sunday morning religious programs and thereby drawing the greatest possible audience. Unlike most independent stations, which leased the rights to show old movies, whenever possible Turner bought films outright so his stations could run the films as often as he wanted.

And run them he did. With a minuscule operating budget and antiquated facilities, the Atlanta station (renamed WTCG for Turner Communications Group) offered its small viewing audience a steady black-and-white diet of dusted-off Hollywood fare – reruns of *Lassie, Father Knows Best* and *Leave It To Beaver* – and professional wrestling's savage ballet.

A significant chunk of the station's advertising consisted of low-cost direct advertising – WTCG hawked everything from wok steamers and priceless recordings "not available in stores" to invincible Ginzu knives, which could cut through a tin can.

NATURAL-BORN SALESMAN

Always a lightning-quick study, Turner immersed himself in the business of running a TV station, poring over every available broadcasting journal and rating book. Of course he also added a peculiar selling and managerial style few had encountered. Despite WTCG's lackluster programming Turner encouraged his salespeople to go after nationwide accounts like Sears that they had little chance of landing. He never faulted them for failing either.

"Never look back," he would tell them about the big fish that got away. "Don't worry about it. Just keep moving forward," according to biographer Goldberg.

Not that he went easy on prospective customers himself. His sometimes bizarre selling tactics rapidly achieved legendary status around the station halls. From jumping onto tables and screaming to kissing a prospect's feet, Turner pulled out all the stops. Facing a particularly stubborn client Turner would fall to the ground yelling, "You're killing me!"

To stem the flow of red out of the Charlotte station he even staged a 24-hour "Beg-a-thon," imploring viewers to send money in to save the station. His act brought almost $50,000 into the struggling station in donations ranging from 25 cents to $100. As much as they questioned his sanity, none of Turner's critics ever denied his prodigious talent for sales.

And it wasn't just his customers who found Turner's come-ons persuasive. Local bankers nearly fell all over each other to lend him money. Turner later described his early strategy for squeezing capital from otherwise reluctant bankers: "What you do is you get a bank, and you borrow all you can borrow," he would tell business groups. "You borrow so much that they can't foreclose on you." He would refer to this as "the secret of my success."

Soon enough the bankers caught on to Turner's schemes and began demanding that he accelerate his payments. Not one to be trifled with, Turner always had a solemn response at the ready. "Keep pressing me," he would threaten, "and I'll just kill myself, and then you won't get anything." Associates said that Turner frequently referred to suicide as the ultimate trump card, the final solution if the house of cards were ever to come crashing down.

TURNER'S BRAVE MOVE

Despite his curious high-profile approach to broadcasting, few outside the Atlanta business community knew who Ted Turner was. All that changed in 1976 when he shelled out $12 million to purchase the woeful Atlanta Braves baseball franchise. WTCG had been carrying Braves games since 1973 and utilizing microwave land lines to spread the station's signal throughout the south to regional cable television operators.

Adding the Braves to his growing empire fit into Turner's overall scheme to own all of WTCG's programming, so he jumped at the opportunity, following his father's credo: "If you really have to have something, it's worth whatever you pay for it."

Typical protocol dictated that owners watch games from lofty private boxes, but Turner opted for a front-row seat. At games he would doff his shirt, drink beer and bask in the sun like any other fan. During his first game as owner the exuberant Turner even ran out onto the field to congratulate a Braves player who had hit a home run.

Braves attendance for 1976 nearly doubled the previous year's draw. Later that year he added the Hawks, Atlanta's pro basketball franchise, to his ownership portfolio. And while the city of Atlanta seemed taken with their unconventional new impresario, the league brass were far less amused by Turner's antics.

When the Braves pursued San Francisco Giants outfielder Gary Matthews in clear violation of league rules, commissioner Bowie Kuhn decided to make an example of Turner. Two weeks after the end of the World Series, Kuhn sent Turner a curt notice, suspending him for the entire 1977 season.

Turner cast himself in the role of martyr and rallied Atlanta's citizenry to his defense. Ignoring an agreement he and the other 25 owners had signed binding them to any decision by the commissioner, Turner took his case to federal court. He knew he had little chance of overturning the suspension, but he really didn't care. He loved the publicity and besides, he had already planned to spend the summer in Newport, Rhode Island, sailing for the America's Cup trophy.

fascinating fact

Turner has collected almost 12 honorary degrees since his expulsion from Brown in 1959.

The Kuhn suspension also revealed another key Ted Turner strategy he would repeatedly use to elevate his power and stature. As Goldberg reported, Turner told Braves publicist Bob Hope: "If you want to get to the top, you've got to argue with the top. If there's a big guy and a little guy in an argument, if the big guy will argue with him, the big guy doesn't come down to his level. The little guy rises up to his level. Now I'm in a fight with Bowie Kuhn. He's big and he's important and he's commissioner. I'm gonna fight him for all he's worth as long as he'll fight back, so I can rise up to his level."

THE NEWSMAN COMETH

Throughout the 1970s Ted Turner's personal stock had steadily risen in the world of cable television operators and station owners. As cable television's most vocal and high-profile advocate Turner spoke to anyone who would listen to him fulminate against the big three networks and tout cable's offerings. In 1976 he testified in front of the House Subcommittee on Communication that the networks had a "virtual stranglehold on what Americans see and think" and that they "do not operate in the public good, showing overemphasis on murder and violence."

At the same time openly envious of the networks' reach and influence, Turner was always on the lookout for ways to muscle one or two of his fingers into their "stranglehold" on the American public. In 1978 Turner decided he was ready to make his assault on the networks. His weapon of choice? An all-news cable channel called CNN.

For friends and foes alike Turner's announcement on May 21, 1979, that in little more than a year he would go on the air with an all-news format was nothing short of astonishing. This, after all, was the man who openly admitted that in his lifetime he had watched fewer than 100 hours of TV news and who had been heard to remark: "I hate the news. It makes people feel bad. I don't want anything to do with the news."

Turner knew he would need credible news professionals on board, however, to make CNN work. His first two hires, Reese Schonfeld, who had previously been running his own not-for-profit news syndication company, and veteran correspondent Daniel Schorr, sent the message that Turner was serious about the project.

Turner left the nuts and bolts work to Schonfeld and directed his attention to raising the station's estimated $30 million start-up costs. With a personal fortune estimated at $100 million and glad to put many of his personal assets up as collateral, Turner had little difficulty obtaining a $20 million line of credit from the First National Bank of Chicago. For additional funds he sold the Charlotte television station to Westinghouse for $20 million, netting a healthy profit on the less than $1 million he had personally put up to buy the station 10 years previously. Time Inc., Scripps-Howard and the Washington Post Company had all considered, then shelved plans for an all-news channel, but Turner considered his venture a sound risk.

"There is risk in everything you do," he told *Newsweek* in 1980. "The sky could fall, the roof cave in; who knows what's going to happen? I'm going to do news like the world has never seen news done before."

As usual, he was right. On June 1, 1980, Cable News Network went on the air and, despite numerous fits and starts, has been on ever since. Although criticized in those early days as the "Chicken Noodle Network," CNN immediately established itself as a player, frequently upstaging the networks with its ability to go live, almost anywhere in the world, at any time. It has been frequently noted that CNN changed news from something that had happened into something that was happening.

On the down side CNN failed to generate advertisers the way Turner had hoped and began operations bleeding at a rate of $1-2 million a month. Operating on a nickel-and-dime budget using inexperienced, nonunion staff, CNN more than once filled its 24-hour-day schedule with on-air flubs and blunders. The exploding light bulb that lit Schorr's clothes on fire and weatherman Stu Siroka's life-and-death struggle with the revolving panels of a weather map were just two of the forehead-smacking gaffes that embarrassed the station's production staff.

Off-camera, Turner felt compelled to sue President Ronald Reagan, Chief of Staff James Baker and all three networks over CNN's exclusion from the official White House press pool.

Paradoxically, exclusion from the press pool indicated just how threatening the big three found the upstart CNN. By late 1981, CBS had opened covert channels to Turner expressing interest in buying CNN from him. While always willing to listen to others tell him what his company was worth, Turner refused the CBS offer. Of greater concern was ABC's response to CNN. In conjunction with Westinghouse Broadcasting, ABC Video announced plans to launch Satellite News Channel, a 24-hour "headline" news channel to compete directly with CNN.

TV NEWS WARS

Westinghouse's deep pockets and existing news-gathering apparatus presented a serious challenge. Never happier than when faced with a crisis, Turner prepared for the fight of his life. Brandishing a favorite Confederate Army saber, he announced to the CNN troops his plans to launch a preemptive first strike, beating Westinghouse to the air with his own headline news service, CNN II. As usual the business press gave Turner little hope of holding off the network challenge. *Forbes* magazine predicted that Turner would likely crash in flames against two such formidable opponents. Turner, however, had other plans.

Understanding the risk-averse nature of most big corporations operating alone, not to mention two working together, Turner planned to hold out to the bitter end, hoping to make the other side blink first.

"After all," he told the media at the time, "we can never lose if we never give up."

At midnight on January 1, 1982 – right on schedule – CNN Headline News went on the air and Ted Turner feted friends to the wee hours at CNN headquarters.

action
PLAN

1 Never give up. As Turner himself says, "We can never lose if we never give up." Any sale you lose to bad timing today, persistence can help you win back tomorrow. When you know you can help your buyers, don't give up on them. How can you keep yourself in your prospects' minds and pursue the sale without being pushy?

2 Act fast. Turner's plan to "think over" his decision to buy WAPO cost him $300,000 and taught him that in business, time is of the essence. If you can get your foot in the door first, you have the first shot at the sale. What can you do to plan more effectively, prepare more thoroughly and make decisions faster to speed up your sales?

3 Seek out new challenges. His boredom with billboards prompted Turner's ventures into broadcasting. His desire to face new challenges also brought him new opportunities. The achievement of one goal gives you a perfect excuse to set another. Where will you look to find new and different ways to test yourself and broaden your horizons?

Response from both cable operators and local network affiliates, who were interested in obtaining syndication rights from Headline News, was overwhelmingly positive.

Meanwhile the cable operators offered ABC a cool reception, noting that the networks had always aggressively opposed the cable industry's growth. After two aborted start-up dates, an abbreviated version of Satellite News Channel went on the air on June 21, 1982, a full 11 weeks after the planned launch date.

Turner was still locked in a life-and-death struggle with the corporate big boys, however, and he worked every angle he could to keep his company afloat. His corporate electric bill fell into such a state of arrears that the electric company threatened to pull the plug on WTBS and CNN. According to then-WTBS advertising executive Gerry Hogan, the entire operation was being sustained by the direct advertising campaign. "If not for the Ginzu knife and the bamboo steamer," he recalled to biographer Robert Goldberg, "for Elvis Presley and Boxcar Willie, we would have been out of business."

> ## fascinating fact
>
> *In 1991, Turner paid $320 million for the animation studio Hanna Barbera.*

Eventually, having spent more than $60 million in start-up costs – twice what they had originally anticipated – to offer a decidedly inferior product, executives at Westinghouse pulled the plug on SNC after only 12 months on the air. Maverick Ted Turner had once again faced the enemy head-on and emerged the winner. Turner Broadcasting acquired SNC for a paltry $25 million and watched its stock soar more than 40 percent.

CNN's coverage of such events as the U.S. invasion of Panama, the Tiananmen Square massacre and the Persian Gulf War cemented CNN as the primary source of late-breaking news for viewers from Peoria to Paris. By the network's 10th anniversary, CNN and Headline News were valued at more than $1.5 billion while CNN alone was generating $150 million in annual operating profit. Superstation WTBS had come into its own as well, becoming the single most-watched basic cable channel in the country.

TAKEOVER TED

In April 1985 Turner officially launched his bid for what was then the biggest network prize of them all: CBS. Predictably, few observers gave the cable tycoon's hostile takeover much chance for success. After all, the TBS guppy, with revenues totaling just $282 million, was attempting to swallow a $4.9 billion CBS whale.

Publicly CBS responded with contempt at the impudent outsider's offer, dismissing him out of pocket. Internally, however, the broadcasting giant scrambled to take on whatever debt necessary – nearly $1 billion – to buy back 21 percent of its own stock, making it prohibitively expensive for Turner to go ahead with his plans.

In a meeting with the TBS board of directors Turner confessed that even he gave the bid only about a 10 percent chance of success. But then Turner revealed his true objectives. He told them that if they failed, the ancillary benefits would outweigh any financial costs. By taking on another much larger foe, Turner Broadcasting would gain greater prestige with advertisers, making it easier to sell advertising on the company's existing stations.

Besides, Turner had no time to lick his wounds; within days of the CBS buyback he had another giant deal in the offing. Turner had always longed for the opportunity to add a movie studio, and its accompanying film library, to the Turner stable.

When financier Kirk Kerkorian came calling with the MGM studio in tow, Turner could hardly conceal his enthusiasm. It took virtually no haggling for Turner to accept Kerkorian's offer of the MGM studio, Culver City movie lot and MGM's library of 3,650 films for $1.5 billion. While industry analysts instantly surmised that Turner had been taken for a ride by the wily Kerkorian, Turner remained enthusiastic about the deal.

"The game I'm in is building assets," he told the *Atlanta Constitution*, "and I've never minded overpaying if I know the values are there."

Three months later, however, just to finance the deal, Turner was forced to sell everything but the library – including the MGM studio and lot and even the MGM lion logo – back to Kerkorian for considerably less than he had paid. In the final reckoning Turner paid about $1.2 billion just for the MGM library,

$200-300 million more than it was worth, according to industry estimates. Worse yet, TBS was still saddled with $1.4 billion in debt.

To extricate himself from this burden without having to sacrifice the precious film library or risk losing control of TBS, Turner went to his powerful colleagues in the cable industry. Preferring the known quantity of Ted Turner to a potential outside interloper taking over TBS, 14 cable companies, including TCI, United Artists and Continental Cablevision, bailed Turner out to the tune of $560 million. The cable barons also leveraged Turner into a shrewd deal. He would retain 51 percent of the company's equity, but he would grant the cable operators seven of 15 seats on the TBS board and give them veto power over any decisions requiring an outlay larger than $2 million.

THE KINDER, GENTLER TURNER

With significantly diminished control of the company's future direction Turner felt justifiably stung by his ventures into the world of high finance and mergers and acquisitions. From that point on Turner's ambitions would be checked by the sober heads on his board of directors. Many outside observers have attributed Turner's more cautious approach to empire building solely to the influence of the board, but other factors have contributed as well.

During the 1980s when Turner and his wife sought professional help for their marital troubles, a psychiatrist convinced Ted to go on lithium for what the doctor diagnosed as a classic bipolar disorder.

Another change in Turner's outlook resulted from his intimate involvement with CNN. As the network's titular head Turner became a bona fide international figure, hobnobbing at various times with luminaries like Fidel Castro, Mikhail Gorbachev and Jacques Cousteau, to name a few.

Turner was disappointed by the Olympic boycotts of the early 1980s so he convinced the Soviets to hold the first Goodwill Games, which have grown to become an international athletic showcase, despite ever-present ridicule from his critics. Sparked by time spent with Cousteau, Turner became deeply interested in issues of population control, nuclear disarmament and, most recently, the global environmental movement. To prove he's serious about his advocacy

Turner even raises 12,000 head of bison on six ranches as an alternative to beef production.

This year Turner aims to expand the Turner Foundation, a nonprofit organization dedicated to green causes, to include a $500 million endowment. He also continues to promote programming and documentaries aimed at increasing awareness about developing global environmental crises.

Recent years have witnessed such successful launches as Turner Network Television (TNT), Turner Classic Movies (TCM), the Cartoon Network, CNN/SI, a 24-hour sports news channel, and a host of international channels. Recovering from the disappointment he felt upon selling the MGM studio back to Kerkorian, Turner now owns his own movie studio, New Line Cinema, as well as a film production company, Castle Rock Entertainment.

FUTURE IMPERFECT

Today, as vice chairman of Time Warner, Turner continues to add to his empire's cable television offerings. Eager as Turner may be to cling to the underdog mantle, the facts betray him. After 30 years spent bucking the conventional wisdom and fending off critics Turner finds himself nestled comfortably in the executive suite of the world's largest media conglomerate.

"You fight the establishment for so long," he concedes, "and one day you wake up and you're part of it." It's enough to make a rebel cry.

But Ted Turner's too busy to cry. Off the record, colleagues claim that he will soon tire of playing second man on the totem pole to Gerald Levin at Time Warner. Assuming he extricates himself from under Levin's thumb, Turner will likely continue his crusade to someday run one of the big three networks. He acknowledged as much recently to a group of TV critics.

"If I died tomorrow," he said, "you know what my tombstone's going to say...'He never got a major network.'"

Lately Turner has again appeared in the press – this time reincarnated as the great cost cutter of the notoriously high-flying Time Warner. Turner, as the largest stockholder in the media behemoth, has reportedly been selling off corporate jets and other holdings in an effort to pare the corporation down to profitable mass.

Many have written Turner's obituary prematurely over the last 30 years — and learned too late that it only encourages him. The Time Warner era proves that he just continues to doggedly pursue his childhood goal to discover what one man can accomplish if he tries hard enough. ▣

From winning the America's Cup to tangling with baseball commissioner Bowie Kuhn, Ted Turner never met a challenge he didn't like. By adapting his unorthodox selling style, charm and resistance to criticism and setbacks, you too can learn to play ball. Your score on the quiz below tells you how well you implement Ted's techniques and how you can model your strategies — and your success — after his.

⑤=**Always,** ④=**Often,** ③=**Sometimes,** ②=**Rarely,** ①=**Never**

1. I understand the importance of timing in sales and try to take action and make decisions promptly.

   ⑤   ④   ③   ②   ①

2. Instead of being intimidated by prospects, I remind myself of my own value and ability and how much I can help them.

   ⑤   ④   ③   ②   ①

3. When I hear criticism or discouraging words, I get even more motivated to be successful.

   ⑤   ④   ③   ②   ①

4. I realize that a fresh or unusual sales approach is often the most effective.

   ⑤   ④   ③   ②   ①

5. Even when prospects turn down my proposal, I keep working on the sale if I know my product is right for them.

   ⑤   ④   ③   ②   ①

6. I enjoy challenging myself and seek out new ways to put my attitude and ability to the test.

   ⑤   ④   ③   ②   ①

Your Total _____

Your Final Score Add your score for each question to get your final score. If you scored:

From 25 to 30 points: You're not afraid to go out on a limb to get the sale. Take your chances, just remember to exercise good judgment at all times. Also, develop Turner's habit of learning all you can about selling, your industry, your customers and your product line.

From 18 to 25 points: Like many other people, you are most comfortable on familiar ground. To reach your potential, though, you should welcome a little fear or anxiety as a sign that you are testing your limits. Learn to think of selling as an adventure, and prepare yourself with information, motivation and training to conquer anything you might face.

Below 18 points: All you have to fear is fear itself. To overcome it, try to understand the reasons behind it. Poor preparation before a call, for example, might make anyone more nervous. After you uncover the causes, confront your fears and, with your manager, develop a plan to overcome them. Present yourself with one small challenge at a time to build your confidence until you feel more in control.

TO SUCCEED FROM SCRATCH, TAKE THESE

LESSONS FROM LILLIAN ON HOW TO MAKE

DECISIONS, MAKE BUYERS FEEL SPECIAL AND LET

THE ENTREPRENEURIAL SPIRIT MOVE YOU.

Lillian Vernon

What do Hillary Clinton, Tipper Gore, Frank Sinatra, Betty White, Steven Spielberg, Loretta Lynn and Arnold Schwarzenegger have in common? In addition to achieving tremendous success in their individual fields, these superstars all number among the millions of customers who have helped build the Lillian Vernon catalog into one of America's most popular and successful direct marketing companies ever.

But as the woman who single-handedly turned a home-based pet project into a multimillion-dollar company knows, Lillian Vernon did not create phenomenal success by catering to the world's rich and famous. Through genuine entrepreneurial spirit, unique sales savvy and an almost superhuman dedication to satisfying every single customer, Lillian Vernon has made her millions by turning the American home into her personal showroom.

From the very beginning, Lillian Vernon has stressed personalizing her products to make each customer feel special. In 1951 as a housewife expecting her first child, Vernon used $2,000 of wedding gift money to purchase a supply of belts and purses and place a $495 advertisement in *Seventeen* magazine offering to personalize orders with her customers' initials free of charge. The response – $32,000 worth of orders from the one ad – would to this day make any direct marketer's mouth water. In her next attempt Vernon added personalized bookmarks and sales more than doubled.

By 1954 Vernon had begun mailing out a 16-page black-and-white catalog offering combs, blazer buttons, collar pins and cuff links – all personalized of

> ## fascinating fact
>
> *Lillian Vernon introduces more than 2,000 new products each year.*

You can't break Lillian Vernon's entrepreneurial spirit. Her self-motivation, work ethic and dedication to customers helped turn $2,000 into a multimillion-dollar mail-order empire. As a salesperson you are also in business for yourself, so follow in her footsteps to foster the entrepreneurial spirit you need to succeed.

Be a self-starter. When you can motivate yourself to action, you hold the key to your own achievement. Vernon had the desire and discipline to build her business without counting on others to get her started and keep her going. Hold yourself responsible for your success, and learn to motivate and discipline yourself to keep moving toward it.

achievement LESSONS

Work your way up. To keep her business afloat, Vernon worked day and night mailing merchandise, writing catalog copy and conducting financial analysis. For success-bound salespeople, long days are the rule rather than the exception. Be willing to work for what you want, and remind yourself often of the great rewards in store for you.

Take your chances. "I take chances," Vernon says, "by acting on my 'golden gut.'" Entrepreneurs know that growth always involves risk, but they are willing to lose so they can eventually win. Learn to weigh risks carefully and to go out on a limb when the potential gains are worth it.

course. In 1956 she stopped operating the business from her kitchen table and moved into a storefront warehouse with a building next door dedicated to monogramming. Not surprisingly, business continued to boom and by 1970, the 19-year-old venture known as the Lillian Vernon Corporation posted its first million-dollar sales year.

After that amazing year, Vernon realized that to continue growing the business she would have to delegate some responsibility and adapt the company to address future concerns. "In the early days," she says, "there was nobody else but me to do the work. During the day I mailed out the merchandise and at night I worked at home doing financial analysis. I did all the buying and wrote the catalog copy; I tried to do it all and it worked pretty well for the first half of my career.

"But after 1970 I was facing a harsh reality. Growing from a million to a multimillion-dollar company involved areas such as finance, list management and computers. So I did what needed to be done and did it quickly – I acted. I filled my ranks with managers from all different walks of life who generally were very savvy to the ways of big business and they almost killed us."

Vernon found that despite their experience these executives couldn't act decisively. Instead of making them into fast-acting visionaries like their new boss, corporate America had taught them to be cautious to a fault.

"Some of the executives I hired just couldn't make a decision," Vernon says. "They took analysis to the point of paralysis. Every major decision had to first be studied by a committee."

From this experience Vernon learned that her success stemmed from time-sensitive decision making and a rapid response to her customers, not from creating committees to mull over every possible course of action. To grow, she realized that the Lillian Vernon Corporation would have to blend the entrepreneurial spirit that built the company into the professional management techniques that must exist in a multimillion-dollar company.

> ## fascinating fact
>
> *Lillian Vernon mails more than 175 million catalogs each year.*

"My mistake," she explains, "was not hiring professional managers; it was letting them work in a nonentrepreneurial fashion. If I've learned anything over the years, it is the importance of drawing from the best qualities of both the entrepreneur and the professional manager. These are the left and right sides of the business brain, and they must harmonize in a healthy corporation."

EXECUTIVE DECISION

To this day the Lillian Vernon Corporation reflects this bullish adherence to the entrepreneurial spirit. The decision-making process is relatively simple. Get the facts, act on your best judgment, then acknowledge and correct any mistakes. Vernon feels that if she has hired and trained the right people to make good decisions, as the company president she has to let their decisions stand without interference from above.

"In the beginning," she says, "I felt like I was sacrificing my career, but it made sense. I encouraged my staff to act on the good instincts I hired them for and keep me posted on their activities. There's nobody to second-guess their decisions or filter information before it reaches my desk. That also means there's nobody to cover up their mistakes. Entrepreneurs must stand or fall on their decisions, and if one of my employees cannot do that we must part company."

action
PLAN

Success Tips from
Lillian Vernon

1. Make time for yourself and your family.

2. Surround yourself with the best people possible.

3. Be open to new ideas and better ways to do things.

4. Don't dwell on your mistakes or setbacks — learn and grow from them.

5. Don't grow without the proper systems and people in place.

6. Be prepared to take risks.

7. Like what you do and like what you sell.

8. Don't try to do it all — delegate.

9. Don't be afraid of technology that can make your business more efficient.

10. Don't spend more money than you have — set realistic budgets and stick to them. Keep your debts manageable.

Although Vernon admits that her management theory may not be so revolutionary as to force Peter Drucker to quit the business, it has led her through uncharted waters and brought unimaginable success. Since 1970 the Lillian Vernon Corporation has grown from two catalogs to eighteen (including one specializing in children's merchandise called "Lilly's Kids"), helped open the Chinese market as a product source, built a national distribution center in Virginia Beach and gone public as the only company on the American Stock Exchange founded by a woman. Since that first million-dollar year in 1970 she has experienced 23 more, the latest being 1993 with record sales of $172.9 million.

What does the future hold for Lillian Vernon? More of the same ground-breaking adventures in untested and untapped direct markets. In 1993 Lillian Vernon products appeared for the first time on an hour-long segment of the QVC Shopping Network and this year the company plans to release its first catalog on CD-ROM. It seems that her true-blue entrepreneurial heart keeps Lillian Vernon driven to create happy customers and keep the competition on the ropes.

"I take chances," she says, "by acting on my 'golden gut.' I try to keep the catalog creative and give my customers the proverbial offer they can't refuse. And most important, I know everything that is going on. There's nothing I hate more than waking up to find that one of my competitors is already doing something that I was planning on. That plus the ability to do things for other people and the opportunity to run a company with high standards of integrity and morality are the motivating factors that keep me going." ▣

Thanks to the integrity, personalized products and great service she offers customers, Lillian Vernon takes orders from everyone. To take more orders of your own, model your success strategy after hers. Put your entrepreneurial spirit and actions to the test and find out how to adjust your skills and attitude so that success has your name written all over it.

⑤=Always, ④=Often, ③=Sometimes, ②=Rarely, ①=Never

1. I can make decisions without taking "analysis to the point of paralysis."
　　⑤　　④　　③　　②　　①

2. I am willing to sacrifice some of my personal time to work the long hours success requires.
　　⑤　　④　　③　　②　　①

3. I understand that customers are the source of my business and I try to meet their needs to the best of my ability.
　　⑤　　④　　③　　②　　①

4. I can take chances and trust my instincts without acting recklessly.
　　⑤　　④　　③　　②　　①

5. I am not satisfied with past successes, but continuously strive to reach new goals.
　　⑤　　④　　③　　②　　①

6. Even if I am employed by someone else, I understand that I work for myself and take responsibility for my own success.
　　⑤　　④　　③　　②　　①

Your Total _____

Your Final Score Add your score for each question to get your final score. If you scored:

From 25 to 30 points: You and Lillian Vernon may be cut from the same cloth. If you are ever tempted to lower your standards of performance or service, remember that your commitment to excellence brought you this far and will ensure your continued success.

From 18 to 25 points: You do well enough until the going gets tough. Remember that success isn't all fun and games. Choose several success role models to inspire you and make their stories part of your routine reading. Motivate yourself by writing down what others expect of you and what you expect of yourself, and review your list regularly.

Below 18 points: You aren't sure what you want or how to get it. Polish your customer service skills by putting buyers before yourself, and identify things that motivate you to take risks and work hard. Set goals for yourself with your manager, and remember that you have only a limited time to achieve the things you want. Start a collection of self-improvement materials to help you get serious about success.

INDEX